PARENTS
ARE LOVERS

PARENTS ARE LOVERS

Fr. Chuck Gallagher, S.J.

IMAGE BOOKS

A DIVISION OF DOUBLEDAY & COMPANY, INC.
GARDEN CITY, NEW YORK

Marriage Encounter Resource Community

Image Books edition published by special arrangement with William H. Sadlier, Inc.
Image Books edition published March 1977

ISBN: 0-385-12697-2
9 8 7 6 5 4

Do you remember?
When we first felt the new dimension of our love.

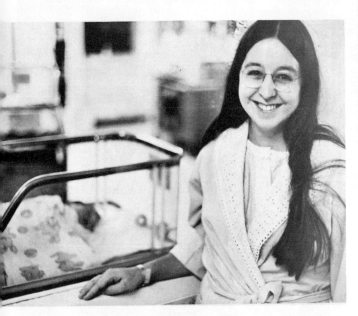

When our love became visible—

and audible . . .

When our back yard was everywhere—

and we kept celebrating our love!

Raising children used to be a simple feat.

New worlds were explored . . .

Up was anywhere,
but gravity was
straight down!

Our love discovered the wheel.

We found a Montana friend who ate out of our hands.

And there was the straw that broke Grandpa's back.

Today we have three expressions of our love.
What fun! What riches! What cause for praise!

What would your snapshots have caught of these important firsts in your life?

movement

tooth

steps

words

kiss or hug

Christmas

birthday party

day at school

report card

lost tooth

broken bone

trip to hospital

communion

two wheeler

driver's license

date

broken romance

graduation

wedding

grandchild

**MEMORIES OF YOUR RELATIONSHIP
ARE THE GREATEST LEGACY
TO LEAVE YOUR CHILDREN.**

Read these pages and consider how you would respond to the questions in view of your own family. No one needs to know your deepest feelings. But if you are familiar with Marriage Encounter and Serendipity programs, you know that the first step to making any relationship better is to be honest and open. Share your answers with one another, and amazing things will happen!

MEMORIES

What memories do you   *Your answer:*
have of your childhood?

Deeply embedded within us all are memories of the experiences and feelings of our childhood. After all, childhood is more than a few years, and they are very impressionable ones. The most outstanding, the most pleasant memory I have of my own childhood is of our family meals. We were all together then—my mom, dad, sister and aunt. The time was a moment for all of us to come together and just enjoy one another. We laughed, sang, told jokes and related what had happened to each of us during the day. Never did we feel more like a family. We were all one. No matter what had happened during the day that upset me, I always looked forward to sitting at the dinner table. The memory warms me—it makes me smile and sparkle even now.

The first memories may not be positive. Maybe the first thing that comes to your mind is something painful. Maybe you saw yourself as an ugly duckling, or very lonely. Maybe it seemed that you weren't the favorite one in your family, or you didn't find the atmosphere in the home warm and accepting at all.

Maybe your memories are of events—the Fourth of July, the Prom—rather than personal relationships. Instead, maybe they focus on school or a camp, which implies something about the home.

In your mind's eye, place yourself back 20 or 30 years and walk through the rooms of your childhood home. See the way the furniture is arranged, look at the decorations on your bedroom wall, imagine the dining room table, the kitchen cupboards, the odors from the kitchen. Then curl up in the place you liked to be most. Who was there with you? Was it the whole family or one particular person? What made it special to you? Let your mother's face come before your eyes—the way she was when you were growing up. What stands out most about her? What qualities do you remember? What good points do you recall? What means most to you in how she acted with you? Recall your dad. Be very conscious of him, how he looked, acted, and spoke. What do you remember most about being with him?

What do you remember about your mother and dad being together? What was their relationship with one another? What did it mean to you? What does it mean to you now? Do you have memories of only one of them? Or do you have memories of each of them—but of their being separate? Or do you recall them as a couple?

Would you say that the memories of your childhood were basically happy memories? In general, looking back over your youthful years, would you say that it was a joy-filled time of life? Certainly that's one of the greatest legacies parents can leave their children. It's part of our joy in life today to look back on our childhood and think of the happiness we had. It's good to think about those days, not that we want to live in the past, but our present is a fulfillment of our past experiences.

It's possible you don't have too many memories of your childhood. Not necessarily because the memories are bad, but because you don't spend any time looking at your early days. That is a mistake. You're depriving yourself of part of your richness. Many of the things that you do now are instinctive reactions to past experiences.

How do your memories   *Your answer:*
affect your life?

Many of us are very conscious of the impact of memories. We can't escape certain experiences that have been traumatic. They may have been positive or negative. We take steps either to make sure the memory never comes alive in our present activities or we constantly yearn for that type of experience again. Sometimes we can be so aware of the big experience that we're not conscious of the other things that happened to us that also have an impact on our present way of living.

Most of us grew up in fairly normal circumstances with the usual joyful and sad moments. Do we recognize how much we're trying to live out in our present lifestyle the home atmosphere we knew many years ago? Or maybe we're trying to do just the opposite, trying to make sure that it's a completely different atmosphere. Many of our decisions, the place where we live, and type of home we have, the food that's on our table and, most especially, the relationship we have with our children, are influenced by our memories.

It can be in very simple things. Maybe we remember how we resented having to eat everything on our plates, so we let the kids leave pretty much what they want to. Possibly we remember how much we wanted to play catch with our father and never could, so we play a lot of ball with our kids.

Our memories also have an impact on how we see ourselves now. If we were lonely as a child, we tend to look on ourselves as lonely now and try to avoid the possibility of loneliness at all costs. If we were an athlete, we still see ourselves as an athlete—even though we may have a 40-inch waist and haven't lifted a basketball for years! At times, of course, we look back on our childhood with rose-colored glasses and see it as a completely carefree time. Now we seem burdened and without enough fun. Actually, though, we created much of our fun in those days. It wasn't really given to us. And it wasn't all that carefree—we had a lot of responsibilities; just as much proportionately then as now.

We may remember our childhood as deprived and be tre-

Oh, for the good ol' days.

mendously concerned about security or making money. On the other hand, we may remember being very successful as a child, and feel discouraged at never having achieved the same success—either in our relationships with people, or in our job or in the home. Or, we can see how far we've come, and we look back and are very pleased with ourselves for having done so well—considering the circumstances. The type of person we are, the car we drive, the clothes we wear, the food we eat, the places we go for recreation, the entertainment we like, the songs we sing, are all very much influenced by the memories we have of our early days.

One of the things we all did when we were youngsters was to picture ourselves in the future. Of course, we realize now that we pictured ourselves as we were then except bigger and stronger and freer—and able to make our own decisions. The reality of who we are now is very much like what we were then. The circumstances may not be what we pictured and some of the romantic details that we included are not present, but we are living out the old saying that the child is the father of the man.

It's important for our self-awareness and our personal appreciation to recognize that our past is greatly affecting how we're living in the present.

How do your memories affect your relationship with your parents?   *Your answer:*

If we're not in frequent physical contact now with our parents we can delude ourselves about our relationship with them. We may think that the distance separating us has cancelled out our relationship, but that's not true. It might be a bad relationship, but it is a relationship! Or we might say to ourselves that under the circumstances we have a very good relationship, but the lack of proximity may cover over the malaise that really exists between us. Maybe we moved to get away from our parents.

Regardless of what the physical circumstances are, what effect do our memories of growing up have on our present relationship with our parents? Often we still see our mother or father as having the same characteristics and attitudes we estimated they had when we were little girls or boys. One of our difficulties is that anything our parents do that smacks of authoritarianism or teaching we pick up immediately and turn off. So, because we're trying to assert our independence, we miss a lot of good advice and direction.

If our memory indicates that their relationship was not very attractive, then we probably try to live a different way. What we discover to our chagrin is that all too often, we've become the kind of woman our mother was or the type of man our father was. We can say to ourselves before marriage, "I'm never going to treat my wife the way my father treated my mother," or, "I won't do to my husband what my mother did to my father." But we often do, and when we recognize these characteristics of our parents coming out in us, we tend to be very harsh and prickly. We don't know how to handle our being the very way we disliked.

Our present relationship with our parents is determined a great deal by how we evaluate the memories we have of our relationship with them. For example, it could be that our mother was sickly in our early years. Now, we either have grown so used to her sickliness that we don't really pay any more attention to her aches and pains, or we treat her as an invalid because that's the way we were trained.

Maybe we remember our parents as not wanting to be bothered with every little detail of our problems. On the other hand, maybe they wanted every "i" dotted and every "t" crossed. The way we deal with them today is in terms of how we remember what they expected of us.

We have very selective memories, and most of us have an

28

inclination to be more mindful of the negative facets of our parents' traits than of the positive ones. We tend to take the good qualities in them for granted and to beware of their defects. How much of our present relationship with them is determined by activities that they've long since given up but which we remember very vividly?

Even though individual instances may stand out, it is the overall type of person we saw our mother or father to be that affects our present-day relationship with them more than anything else. We may have seen them as stiff and unbending, as kindly and understanding, or as busy. We may have looked on them as joy-filled or as serious. Whatever we noticed their predominant characteristic to be modifies our responsiveness to them today.

How do your memories affect your relationship with your children?   *Your answer:*

It is evident that memories which had a strong negative impact on us are not going to be the ones we want our children to have. If we remember something that broke our hearts, we'll do almost anything to make sure that the same thing doesn't happen to our children. It might be that we didn't have any social life when we were kids, and the loneliness is etched sharply within us. The lonely feeling may be symbolized in a single incident such as missing a prom or sitting alone on a bus, but it affects all sorts of decisions that we make about our children. It's almost certain that we're going

Our children will have "warm" winter memories!

to be compulsive about making sure that our children have a lot of opportunities to make friends. We're going to really insist upon their being active all the time with other children, whether it's good for them or not.

We may believe that our parents controlled our lives too much, so we give our children a lot of freedom. In all probability, though, we're still very controlling parents.

On the other hand, if we remember our childhood as being happy, we're going to want our children to do the same things as we did, to have the same type of circumstances that made us happy. It's going to be difficult for us to adapt ourselves to the personal needs of our children and not assume that what made us happy is automatically going to make them happy.

We are also influenced by our clearly remembering things we wanted but didn't have. These are not necessarily material things. It could be religion, an education, an opportunity to travel, a chance to play a musical instrument, certain books, or just a simple thing like standing on the street corner hanging around with a crowd. We're going to want to make sure that the unfulfilled dreams we had don't remain just dreams for our children. But our children may not be drawn to those particular things, and imposing our dreams upon them creates a tense situation.

We may have had very close family experiences, and we cherish those memories. We had opportunities to express ourselves and to experience a warm family relationship. For example, we may remember family meals as magical times. Not every meal, of course, but many of them. The memory of the overall tone enables us to make meals special for our children.

The memory of a gentle, understanding father or mother who always had a willing ear, who was always eager to comfort and console, may help us when we find it difficult to listen to our children.

Looking back over our childhood may remind us of the special little presents and the cookies and treats we were given. This may lead us to do the same things for our children. We may recall the wonderful moments when Daddy came into the house from work. What fun we had! What a joy it was! As our kids jump on us, that memory can take the slump out of our shoulders and the tiredness from our legs.

Our parents may have made many sacrifices and assumed heavy burdens in order to give us what they considered a full life. If that is our strongest memory, then we may adopt the role of being providers and caretakers of our children rather than having a deep relationship with them.

The parents we experienced have taught us to be the parents we are no matter what the appearances are. If our parents considered us a duty and a responsibility, then we are likely to consider our children the same way. We're going to look on parenthood as a job, one that is a very important job and one that has lifelong ramifications, but still a job. And we'll feel that our doing of the job is going to be pretty well accomplished by the time our children are 21. So, we actually give our children a feeling of temporariness.

Memories are dynamic. They do not simply determine how we act in individual circumstances or in specific areas of parenthood. They create an atmosphere in our relationship with our children. The atmosphere may be one of strictness or lenience, of dutifulness or permissiveness, of calmness or tenseness, of happiness or sadness. Our memories can create an environment in which we are dependent upon our children for our self-satisfaction in life.

It's our memories that determine the kind of parents we are, whether those memories are plus or minus. We make our decisions on the basis of what it was like "when." We can kid ourselves and say, "We don't do that—we're very modern parents and we've decided to do the good things that were not done for us and to avoid doing the bad things that were done for us." But that's precisely it! It's on the basis of the memories of the effects of our parents' decisions that we make our present decisions.

That's not bad in itself. But we better sort out our memories and really take a look at them. Maybe we have distorted them. Maybe we should see which memories are having the biggest impact on our present decisions, and what effect they are having on our children.

How do your memories affect the decisions you make regarding your children?

Your answer:

Whether we think so or not, our memories influence the decisions we make. We tend to kid ourselves, thinking we decide all sorts of things: the allowance our children will have, who we will encourage them to have as friends, the hour they are to come in, whether they'll have a bicycle, whether they can play sports, what kind of school we send them to, what ambitions we have for them in the future, the type of clothes they wear. The list is endless and could go on and on. We really honestly believe that we decide all these things on the basis of principles that we apply in accordance with what the particular circumstances call for right now. But in actuality, the strongest single factor influencing our present decisions with our children is how our parents' decisions affected us.

Often enough, we explain our decisions on the basis of "things are different today." But that's usually applied when we're allowing the children to do something we wanted to do and were restricted. On the other hand, if we have very strong, joyful, positive memories of our childhood, we definitely want our children to have those experiences—even though things are different today.

The stronger motive in making different decisions than our parents did is not the changing times, but our dissatisfaction with the past.

However, it might well be that a decision our parents made was correct, but they applied it improperly. Therefore, what should be changed is the way the decision is applied rather than the actual decision itself. For example, our parents maybe gave us pocket money and it caused a lot of difficulty. Other kids were always scrounging off us and we knew we

Saturdays meant playing ball.

were being taken advantage of. Since we weren't mature enough to handle the situation and say no to them, we were very unhappy with ourselves. In order to keep our children from having that problem, we may be tempted to not give them much money at all. A better way of approaching it could well be to give them some money, but then to discuss with them exactly what's happening with the money.

Because we are inclined to think of our children as being little images of ourselves, we feel that anything we recall favorably must naturally be something that's going to turn them on, that something we remember as making us fearful or disappointed or disillusioned is going to make them feel the same way. If we were at our best in sports, then we expect

35

our son to shine in sports. If a woman treasures the memory of dressing up and having her hair specially combed and feeling wonderfully feminine, she will want to treat her daughter as though she likes the same things regardless of what that girl's personality is. A haunting memory of being out of style can lead us to almost force our children to conform to whatever is popular at the moment. An ecstatic memory of riding a roller coaster can lead us to insist that even our most timid youngster take the "fun" ride.

It could be that our compulsion for having separate rooms for our children comes from our recollection of sharing a bedroom with brothers or sisters and not liking the invasion of privacy or the conflicts of personality. Yet one of the things that's starting to come out through some studies is that siblings who sleep together in their childhood have a special, continuing relationship, different and much better than with the rest of the family.

Snack foods are prevalent in our homes. We even know the snacks aren't the best thing to have around but we keep them available. Why? Probably it comes from the infrequency and unavailability of snacks in our own lives, and how special they were to us when we did get them.

Our fearfulness of seeming authoritarian or of even taking a definite stand may come from our remembering how we reacted when our parents "laid down the law."

Memories of our mother or father feeling burdened with us, of having sacrificed their potential and their personal ambitions because of us, can make us determined to free ourselves from our children.

Frequently we feel that our whole lifestyle—the decisions we make, the goals that we have for our children—is completely different from that of our parents. That may appear to be true because the externals are different. We have television; they had radio. We have planes; they had trains. Yet we may still have an atmosphere that is exactly the one we want to avoid! Maybe we grew up in a home where our parents felt they had all the answers and they were very free in giving them to us. Now we're determined that we're not going to be that way with our kids, so we have none of the answers. We just listen. Anything they happen to come up with is perfectly all right with us. It's really the same atmosphere. In either case the person is not being responded to. Issues are the subject in the first case. Our not wanting to appear dictatorial is the subject in the second case. The child is ignored in both instances.

The most significant fact about the impact of memories is that the negative memories tend to have the strongest influence. That's understandable because we're more responsive to pain than pleasure and therefore very determined to avoid it.

When we are making decisions based on the pleasant memories of the past, we often focus in on the workings of such events as family dinners, parties or holiday times. It would be better to concentrate on exercising the personal qualities of our mother or father, making sure that they are available for our children. We tend to excuse ourselves by saying, "I'm just not that kind of a person," but we can be. If we decide to be! We can just as well develop qualities that we recall from the past as we can implement practices.

How do your memories affect the way you react to your spouse's relationship with your parents?   *Your answer:*

We expect everybody to have the same reaction we have to a person who is close to us. So if we have a good relationship with our mother, we expect our husband or wife to have a good relationship with her and to the same degree. If we're having a struggle with our father, we don't expect our spouse to really like him.

If the husband or wife had a great deal of misunderstanding through the years with one of the parents, but the spouse finds that person easy to get along with and has developed a good relationship, there can be friction between the husband and wife. The one not having a good relationship with the parent may feel that the spouse is not being supportive or understanding. Furthermore, there can be an undercurrent of jealousy. The one sees the relationship that he would like to have with his parent, and the spouse has it.

We may recall our parents liking one of our brothers or sisters better than they liked us. If our husband or wife has a good relationship with the in-laws, it brings up bitter memories. We may try to step between them and not allow the good relationship to continue.

Also, we may have counted very much on our parents for advice. We recognized they had very good heads on their shoulders and a lot of common sense. We had an instinctive trust in the direction they would advise us to go. Now we tend to look for our spouse to have that same trust in our parents. If he doesn't, it can interfere with our relationship. Or, we may have been striving for independence all our life long, wanting to stand on our own feet. We've trained ourselves not to listen to our parents. We don't understand why our partner takes the trouble to listen to them, let alone agree with them.

Recollections of how our mother and father treated one another may set us up to expect certain things in our husband or wife. We may be constantly comparing our spouse to one parent or the other. We may have these expectations without ever expressing them. We experienced our parents' relationship all the time we were growing up, so we think it is a natural way to act. As a result, the poor spouse is condemned without even knowing what the crime is. We may remember a great peace in our home, which may or may not have existed. If our spouse runs into any conflicts with parents, then we tend to have difficulty with our spouse.

Our spouse's relationship with our parents can also cause a negative reaction in the relationship we have with our parents. If our spouse and our parents are on friendly terms, we might think our parents are taking our husband's or wife's side too much. Or the other way, if there is a conflict between spouse and parents, we might have hostile feelings every time we see our parents.

How many good husbands and wives make each other terribly nervous when they're about to visit their parents? They warn each other to be on guard. Each person becomes unnatural. The uncomfortable situation may be caused by a casual comment that a father passed at a dinner table many years before, or a remembrance of the initial reaction the mother had to the girl's date or to the boy's fiancée.

We might have memories of our father speaking about what a man or a woman should be like. If we don't see our spouse as fulfilling what Dad saw as ideal, we presume that Dad doesn't like our partner. Or, we might remember the way our mother kept the house or cooked the meals or treated the children. If our wife does things differently, we presume that our mother disapproves.

Just such simple things as deciding a present or who pays for a meal out can well be determined by what we recollect of the way our parents did things.

When we look on all these influences on our lives, they may seem silly, horribly silly. Or it may seem that these situations didn't really happen. But when we examine ourselves, we discover that our relationships are affected. We have fallen into these traps. It's not easy to avoid them. First of all, we have to recognize that we're in them. Secondly, we have to be willing to be open both with our parents and our spouse. We need to discuss our feelings, express our expectations, and work together to have a fresh outlook.

How do your memories affect the way you react to your spouse's relationship with the children?

Your answer:

In the relationship our spouse has with our children, we are probably expecting him to live up to the way our mother or father acted with us. We are influenced by the pleasant memories of the times our parents spent with us or the special qualities they had that we appreciated so very much. We look for those particular qualities in our spouse, and if they're not there—or if they're not there to the degree that we remember them—then we consider our spouse to be lacking. It is likely our husband or wife has all sorts of other beautiful qualities that have a tremendous impact for good upon the children, but we don't even notice them.

For example, our father might have been really great at roughhousing and at playing ball with us. Our husband is less inclined toward physical activities but creates an atmosphere of warmth in his own way. We think our children are deprived. Maybe our mother was very imaginative in thinking up games for us, and our wife just isn't that way. She has her own qualities of interest and understanding in the children, but we bypass those because we're looking for a certain kind of creativity.

It's one thing to share what meant a great deal to us growing up and to help our spouse to develop those qualities because they are good in themselves; it's an entirely different thing to measure him or her against those standards. To share is a plus, an added richness in the home. To measure is a minus. It's looking at what our spouse doesn't have and judging him or her as inadequate.

Sometimes our memories cause us to accept a lesser relationship than we need have. Our early home life may have had some very negative things that we remember in our relationship with our mother and father. As long as those things are not present in our home we're so relieved that we don't look for anything else. Maybe our father or mother had a violent temper, or one or the other was never around, or possibly one of them didn't seem to take too much interest in us children, or they were penny pinchers or too demanding. So, we deliberately tried to choose a husband or wife that did not have those drawbacks. As long as those problems don't show up in the relationship with us or the children, then we're quite satisfied and we back off from wanting anything more.

In our growing up, if we experienced hurt from one of our parents, we may try to protect our children from our spouse as soon as we see any possibility of a similar experience. Sometimes we don't have to even see evidence of it. We have such vivid memories that we stand between our children and our spouse. We don't allow any real relationship to even begin. That's the worst thing that can happen to our children. It's better to risk the possibility of hurt. Hurt is going to occur in any relationship no matter how good the people are or how hard they try not to let it happen. The biggest hurt comes from the absence of relationship. That's what leads to loneliness, a sense of self-rejection and alienation. Therefore we cannot allow our memory of personal pain to permit us to isolate our children from our husband or wife.

We may not be standing between our children and our spouse in all areas. We may be restricting the relationship between them to certain narrow areas: studies, dating, heart-to-heart talks, or the future. We need to step out of the way.

How do your memories affect the way you react to the decisions your spouse is making with the children?

Your answer:

Our recollections of the decisions our mother and father made definitely influences the way we react to our spouse's decisions. We may look back on our mother and father and think they were very, very strict. Any strict action of our spouse makes us over-react. We want to be sure that our children do not have strict parents. Or it may be that our parents were always saying yes. They pretty much let us do anything we wanted to and it came across as indifference. We felt they really didn't want to get involved, that they didn't care about us. We've decided that that's not going to happen to our kids. We're going to make sure they know they are cared for. We will take the responsibility of saying no sometimes. So, when we want to say no and our partner is saying yes, we tar him with the same brush we apply to our parents.

Some families make a great deal about presents. Maybe there were presents for everything: birthdays, Christmas, Easter, Baptismal days, Confirmation days and so on. We can recall what fun it was to open presents. If our husband or wife is not inclined to make such a big deal about presents, thinks they're overdone and wants to cut down on them, we may have difficulty understanding the value that's being suggested. We're allowing memory to come between us instead of having that memory support our present situation and add to the richness that's in us.

Memories can cause a lot of take-it-for-granted-ness in us. This can lead to friction between husband and wife because both of them have memories and both of them have assumptions. We may have memories of a certain lifestyle or a certain atmosphere in our childhood home that we unconsciously expect to be present in our home now. Because we're so sure of it, our spouse doesn't say anything about it. But it's not really the way he or she would like to live.

We may be trained by our past experience to believe that there are certain decisions that are the mother's and others that are the father's. We may be taken aback if our husband or wife seems to be intruding into an area that we consider our own, or we may feel burdened if we're asked to enter an area that we had always considered to be the partner's.

Our memory bank tells us that the woman is better equipped and more competent than the man to make decisions about the children. Consequently both the husband and wife are liable to consider the wife to be superior as a parent, to be more in touch with the children. The terrible result of that kind of thinking is that the child is being raised more by one parent than by both.

We need to evaluate where we are. We're a couple—with children. We need to make "couple" decisions.

What memories will your children have of you 20 years from now?   *Your answer:*

It is natural and understandable that parents want to be remembered fondly by their children. But it is as much for the sake of the child as for the parent. The child's memories need to be pleasant and very positive. Of course, we should not always be agreeing with the child or always giving in to the child or doing what the child wants so that they can remember a calm household. (As a matter of fact, that type of acquiescence can be self-defeating. The child can recognize that we were too dependent on his approval and didn't love him the way that he should have been loved.)

The pleasant, positive memories are the most rich when they revolve around a child's relationship with both parents—together. When he knows the importance that we have to one another. When he can look back and know that he was understood and really cared for, reached out to, and we all had a real sense of belonging to one another. It has very little to do with material things or the activities that we engaged in, and a great deal to do with the rapport that was established. These memories are accomplished more by communication, listening, revealing ourselves and letting the child know who we are as persons than they are by any other technique or experience.

What do we think our children will say about us in 20 years when they sit down with their own children and describe what Grandma and Grandpa were like when Mommy and Daddy were youngsters? How will they describe us as persons? What qualities will come to their minds? What defects of ours will they think of, even if they don't mention them aloud?

It would be easy enough to answer these questions if we'd just had a fight with one of our children. We're sure to think that our child is going to be very negative about us. That's not necessarily true. Even if we've gone through a fairly extended difficult time, it doesn't mean that our children's memories of us are naturally going to be bad. Instead, they may be impressed with our taking a stand against what they really know to be wrong! We could also feel that because we've done all the right things by our children, made all the right decisions and done everything that we thought was the right thing to please them, that they're going to have good memories. That's not necessarily true, either.

Our children's memories of us are apt to be decided on the basis of how much they considered themselves understood, how free they were to talk to us, how much time we spent with them, did they delight in being in our presence? They'll remember if their friends were welcome and whether or not the home was sort of a center for the neighborhood. Sometimes we can think that as long as our children are our children and we let them talk a lot, that's enough. But in any human relationship, it's got to be more than that. One of the key questions we can ask ourselves is, "How have we revealed ourselves to our son or daughter?" Unfortunately in many homes, we hide ourselves from our children. We don't want them to see our weaknesses; we want them to consider us as being in complete control, knowing how to handle our lives, making decisions without a hassle and so on. So we come across to our children as inhuman. In our "perfectness," our parent-child relationship is unequal, not very satisfying, and definitely not leading to happy memories.

In 20 years or so when our children sit down with their

children and start to talk about us, what will be the first thing that automatically comes into their minds? Will it be that we made a lot of money, or that we were respected, or that all sorts of people liked us, or that we were persons of great integrity, or that we had great natural abilities and skills, or that we were very active in organizations and civic affairs? Or will it be something that centers around who we were to them as persons and what our relationship was together? Will the warmth in their words fill the room as they talk about how close they always felt to us?

Will your children's   *Your answer:*
memories be ones that
you wanted to give them?

Have we deliberately sat down with our husband or wife and talked about what memories we want our children to have of us? Have we figured out how we're going to create those memory tracks in them? All too often a lot of mistakes happen by default. It isn't that we consciously and deliberately choose to do the wrong thing; it's simply that we don't think of what the right thing is to do. We do to a degree. We plan our certain days or deeds to give the children a good time. They'll remember that we took them to Disneyland or to the beach in the summer, or that we gave them special presents one Christmas that were really too extravagant.

Individual, isolated incidents and accidental happenings can create great moments of closeness between us, but leaving memories pretty much to chance is risky. It is better that we deliberately and consciously set out on a campaign to create the memories that our children will have of us. The memories are terribly important for them in their relationship with one another as husbands and wives and in their relationship with their children.

If we look ahead and see how we want them to talk about us to our grandchildren, we can make decisions accordingly. When you come right down to it, memories, in a sense, are the end product of parenthood. Consequently, if we look at the end product and then see what ways we can use to develop it most effectively—the memories we want our children to have—it's going to help us in our relationship with them now. We would never think of leaving their education to chance. We would feel very guilty if we had an opportunity to leave them money and did not take advantage of it. But when it comes to memories we tend to just let them happen. They are not an ego trip; they are not intended to be for our sake, to have our children remember us well so that we feel good. It is a very real, flesh and blood, honest approach to being parents. No matter how much money we may leave our children, no matter how good an education we may give them, the greatest legacy that we can ever leave our children is memories of us.

How will your children's memories affect your grandchildren?   *Your answer:*

We recognize how strong an impact our memories have on the way we're treating our children. We also have a hand in creating the atmosphere for the home in which our grandchildren will grow up.

The memories that our children have can give our grandchildren a sense of roots. Memories are what make us present to our grandchildren. We cannot guarantee that we are going to be physically present to our grandchildren, because our children may move far away from us—or we may have passed on. We are apt to be present to them only through the memories of our children.

But even in our direct dealings with our grandchildren, memories play a role. Though most of us are not with our grandchildren often and regularly, we are consistently with them through the memories that their parents share with them. If not, the relationship is a shallow one. Grandma and Grandpa come in, drop a few presents, get caught up on the news of school activities and little triumphs and then walk out again—to be forgotten until the next time there's an occasion for a present.

The relationship that our children have with us is going to affect the attitudes with which our grandchildren come toward us. With indifference, with timidity, nervousness or fear or—best of all—with warmth, enthusiasm and eagerness.

The more positive our children's memories are, and the more deeply they're embedded, the more frequently the memories will be brought up in conversation and the more often we are going to be present to our grandchildren.

What adventures we had every summer!

How important is it
to share with your
children the fond
memories you have
of your spouse?

Your answer:

One of the greatest resources from which our children can draw is our relationship with our husband or wife, and part of our present relationship is our past relationship. Have we told our children how we met and what we first thought of one another? The details of our first date and our thoughts afterwards will fascinate them. Children find it difficult—if not impossible—to imagine their parents as ever being young. We can help them to be aware of our dating days, the places we went, what pleased us, what we said to one another, what our favorite song was, what kind of date was most meaningful to us, what subjects we talked about, and what subjects we avoided talking about.

We can tell our children how the all-important proposal took place and what the response was. The circumstances will intrigue them. All the little details of the engagement ring, how it was bought and what it meant when it was first put on the finger and what was said at that time. All the preparations for our wedding and the comments of the relatives and friends and what our hopes and fears were before we got married. The details of the wedding dress and the flowers and the bridesmaids and the ushers and everything including the sending out of the invitations and even what we were thinking about as we waited at the head of the aisle or walked down the aisle. They'll even want to hear about the early days of our marriage. All the particulars are important for our children.

All too often they only see us at the present moment. They don't see the history that we have together and how important it is to our relationship right at this moment. It's a great experience for our children to know that we were once 20 and that we fell in love and that we laughed and giggled and went to dances, that we were a joy and a heartache to one another, and that our days were fused with a consciousness of each other. We can give this gift to our children. We are depriving them if we don't talk about those early days.

The greatest fairy stories in the world can't compare with just telling stories about Mommy and Daddy. There really is a Prince Charming in the home, a far better one than in the storybooks. There is a Sleeping Beauty that was brought alive by a kiss. Children never hear too much about the first kiss or about the engagement, or the wedding day. It may be very hard to believe, but there is a vibrancy and a reality in the stories about ourselves that nothing else can ever match.

How important is it to share with your children the memories you have of them?

Your answer:

Sometimes we take out our children's baby pictures and tell funny little stories about what was happening when they were taken. Those experiences are very precious, and our children laugh and giggle and treasure them in their hearts. The more we talk about the early days of their lives, the more we enrich them. The more we show them how precious they are to us by remembering a great deal about them, the more they are going to recognize that they're cared for and thought about constantly.

Unfortunately, we usually go over the past only when relatives or friends or grandparents are in. (That's one of the graces that grandparents bring to a family—they talk about the past, and not just about their own past, but about the past of our children!) We have to make it often.

One of the best stories to tell our children can be of their birth. How we looked forward to having them. How they

More than just play money was exchanged around our family table.

were an expression of our love. What went through our minds the last month of pregnancy with each of them. The fears and the worries about their health and physical wholeness. The hopes that we had for them. The eagerness that was in our hearts for the birth to take place. How we couldn't wait to see them!

Children love to know the exact details of their births. Where they were born. How Daddy drove Mommy to the hospital. What he was thinking about and what she was thinking about. What time of day it happened. How long it took for them to be born. What they looked like. What the reaction was of Mommy and Daddy to first seeing them and holding them and touching them. How much they weighed. How long they were. What color hair they had, if any. Our children want to hear what the relatives said and did when they came to see the baby in the hospital. The hustle and bustle of coming home from the hospital. The first day home and what each of the other children said and did when they saw the new little baby. How they all wanted to hold him. For our children to learn of their early moments—and what everyone's first impressions of them were—is a magnificent, exciting experience.

Principles and guidelines:
1. *Memorable moments are often those in which there is a sense of closeness.*
2. *Memorable moments don't always just happen; we can help make them happen.*
3. *Everyday experiences can be memorable; these often have a great potential to be memory-full.*
4. *Events in which we parents are present to our children will be memorable to them.*
5. *The more responsive and attentive we are to our children at any given time, the more life-giving the memories of those moments will be.*
6. *Our children's fondest memories will be of the times they are listened to and understood and know they are loved.*
7. *It is meaningful to share our memories, especially the good ones, of our parents, of one another and of our children.*

51

MORE THAN ANYTHING LISTENING TO YOUR CHILDREN CONVEYS LOVE, UNDERSTANDING, ACCEPTANCE.

2

LISTENING

**What kind of parent
do you want to be?**   *Your answer:*

The responsibilities and obligations of being a parent seem to
be completely obvious. But what are they, really? What are
our goals? What are we looking for in ourselves as parents?
Many people look ahead to see what they should be providing
for their children. Maybe we should look back and see what
we most enjoyed in our parents' relationship with us! Do we
remember the moments of closeness, of understanding, of tenderness, the family warmth.

When we're thinking about our children and what we
should do for them, we often think in terms of their educa-

tion, their social development, the use of their talents, their skills in music, dancing, games and what have you. We might think of the fun they should have, but we tend to think of it in terms of their going to the playground or to a party—activities outside the home.

Isn't it also true that we look on parenthood as a series of services that we are expected to perform for our children? And we see ourselves as "the mother," "the father"—roles to be played?

I remember the boy Al, who was on my freshman basketball team. He was a typical example of a boy who had everything. His mother and dad were the perfect parents. They had money and used it well. They gave Al a beautiful bike, nice clothes, his own stereo with lots of records, music lessons, good food, excellent medical attention—everything. He had a basketball hoop hung on the garage roof and his father even shot a few with him after supper each night. His mom and dad attended all his Little League games. They went to all the parent-teacher conferences. But Al, with all of that, was a moody kid. He didn't feel understood by his parents. Whenever Al heard his parents talking, it was never really about him, but what they should do for him; how they should live up to their responsibilities as parents. He saw himself as a burden—as a part of their duties—and didn't see himself as contributing anything to their life. He wasn't really part of their lives.

On the other hand, Tony just enjoyed life. His parents never went to PTA. They were too embarrassed by their clothes. His father had to work and couldn't get to his games, and his mother thought sports were just for men. His father was too physically tired to play with Tony when he came home. Homework was beyond them, so they left it up to him. But they delighted in Tony. They enjoyed having him around. He wasn't a responsibility, he was a pleasure. It seemed his parents weren't doing the things good parents are expected to do, but they did what was most important. They made him feel special. Tony knew his dad bragged about him at work and that his mom and dad liked to have him around. He had it made.

We will, if we sit down to talk about it seriously, recognize that parenthood is much, much more than doing "right things." There's an emotional and personal involvement with the children to consider. However, on a day-to-day basis, the goals we're striving to reach are pretty much exercised in terms of activities. Are we apt to think the personal dimensions of parent and child relationships take care of themselves? Actually, it's more likely that the other needs of our children will be taken care of—or won't loom so large on the horizon as they do—if we focus in on the personal dimension of relationship.

Do you believe it's up to you to determine your children's future happiness?   *Your answer:*

It has become fashionable in our society to put the full blame for every aberration and human failing on the parents—especially the mother! This puts a tremendously heavy burden on parenting. But there are all sorts of other aspects of a child's development, including the most important of all—free will. So, just as we can't claim the credit for the success and development of a boy or girl, we need not take the blame for the failure. When we do, we tend to be all over our children, smothering them, because we're afraid we are going to fail.

We have to get away from our compulsive and fearful attitude toward being a parent. We can look on it as an opportunity, and a life-filled one! We can be freer with ourselves and with our children, because there is another side of the coin. The investment of our personhood in our children can be a tremendous endowment. Just like a material endowment, they can throw it away, misuse it or just let it stagnate, but it's there for them to use properly if they wish. It should be provided. There's no question but that we do have an impact on our children's happiness in the days to come—the personal happiness even more than the material happiness. We can make sure that this occurs if we are concerned most of all with our personal relationship with them.

What would make you a success as a parent?   *Your answer:*

If you could look into the future and see your children 20 or 30 years from now, what qualities would you want to see to indicate that you had done a good job?

Naturally we have many ambitions for our children and we want to see them a success in all areas of their lives. But what do we consider to be of prime importance for them to have meaningful lives?

Probably the best way to find out is to examine what we talk about to our husband or wife when we discuss our children's future. What are we aiming for? Why are we putting in all this effort and all this love? Is it because we want them to get a good job and support a family? Have a fine education so they can enjoy some of the nicer things in life? Be self-reliant so they can stand on their own two feet and make their way in life? Have principles and stand by them? Or possibly our ambition is that they be self-disciplined or able to handle themselves in all sorts of circumstances and not just give way to their inclinations. Maybe our ambitions for our children are more amorphous. We just want them to have a nice family and live a good solid life in which they can be happy.

All these hopes for our children are good and valid ones. They have importance, but something is missing. Truthfully, what we should be all about as parents is simply to love our children and to teach them to be lovers.

To be a "lover" is not a silly, soupy, nicey-nice type of thing. It includes principle and discipline and self-reliance and education and capability and, above all, the ability to love and be loved. More important than anything in the lives of parents is to develop a love relationship with their children and to teach their children how to participate in a love relationship—first and foremost with them and then with others, most especially their husband and wife and children when they have their own homes. Any person who loves and is loved enjoys a successful life, no matter what the circumstances are.

So, without any guilt feeling at all, the number one priority of any mother and father can be the love that's in the home!

What is the key to love?   *Your answer:*

When you talk about the need for love in the home, of course everybody nods his head. There's nobody who would quarrel with that statement. Unfortunately love is something everybody agrees with but, in all probability, defines differently. To some, love is a feeling, a sense of warmth and closeness and instinctive responsiveness toward someone. To others, love is a series of activities—doing all the right things for a person who is called a beloved. To still others, love is being loved. They're thinking almost exclusively of how others, or someone, makes them feel. It's really what they're getting out of another person, rather than what they're putting into a relationship.

They sympathized with us over taxes!

When we talk about loving our children, we're often talking only about doing the right things for them, of taking the proper care of them or making sure they have everything that's necessary for their physical, material, psychological and spiritual well-being. But love for our children has to go beyond these things. If the parent-child relationship is not just to be a custodial one, but a true, love relationship, then we have to start talking about personhood and the communication of personhood to one another. Actually there is no love without communication. We may give loving service to another person, but it may be more of a response to my feelings or to my principles rather than a caring for the other person.

In many homes there is very little communication of personhood between parents and child. On either side. This is even true in families that seem to be getting along with each other pretty well. There are many children growing up whose parents don't really know them and they, unfortunately, don't really know their parents. We may know a lot about each other, but that doesn't necessarily mean we know one another in the depth of our beings. We may even be talking a great deal to one another and yet not necessarily be communicating. (One of the ways of hiding ourselves from one another is by silence. Another way is by talking. We talk a lot about things, not about ourselves.)

Isn't it incredible that whenever we examine our qualities as parents we look to our generosity or our self-sacrifice, whether we lose our temper with our children or whether we spend enough time with them in their activities or attend their plays and sports events? We look to see if our children seem to be developing normally in all the various stages of their lives, but hardly ever do we ask ourselves, "Do our children really feel understood?" or, "Do we feel understood by them? Could we talk to them about anything that's in our hearts?" Let's try. For isn't the first and foremost qualification for a love relationship between parents and children the ability to communicate personhood?

Do we even know that it's expected of us to reveal ourselves personally? Or that we have a right to look for understanding from our children? Can they understand us as real flesh-and-blood persons with feelings and desires and worries and concerns and a real yearning to be responded to? Of course they can. Our children have amazing capabilities—far more than we can imagine. Let's try them out!

Do you have a double standard communication: one for your children, one for your spouse?   *Your answer:*

We tend to look at our children as Little Leaguers and ourselves as Major Leaguers. We think they have problems and concerns and worries, but that theirs are so much less than our own! Yes, we're going to pay attention to them because they're troubled, but we don't really take the problems nearly so seriously as our children do. We think we know what the answers are and, yes, we'll try to be patient.

So, all too often we just sort of fix the child up. It's like putting a Band-Aid on a sliver. We don't listen to them the way they want to be listened to. If, for example, they've lost a friend, we tell them, "Your feelings will pass. You'll find other friends." But if we were to lose a friend, someone who is very dear to our hearts, would we accept an answer like that? Instinctively we tend to look on what happens to our youngsters as different because, "After all, childhood friendships are broken all the time." For that matter, so are adult friendships!

It's really a problem of equality. We certainly are not expected to look on our children as equal to us in prudence or experience or self-reliance or in the ability to make broad-ranging decisions, but we can look on them as equal to us as persons. They have an equal capacity to be hurt. They are just as able to reveal themselves as we are—and to listen. They have every bit as much personhood as we have. It's hard for us to see this sometimes. We tend to think they are not really complete yet.

Because we think of our children as somehow "less" than we are, we treat them differently than we want to be treated, especially when it comes to communication. We postpone a time to talk with them because what they want to talk about isn't important in our eyes. Yet we recognize that frequently what we want to talk about with our husband or wife may not be important, but we are! We have a need to communicate. We expect our spouse to respond not so much to the topic—as to us. Sometimes we don't want answers; we just want to be heard.

Sometimes I get down. A lot of times there are specific reasons for it. I misread someone; I put my foot in my mouth, or someone misunderstood me. There are even occasions when I'm down for no discernible reason. In either case, it helps just to talk it out. But I hate it when someone tries to tell me I shouldn't feel down—or that I'll feel better soon. I don't want advice and I certainly don't want to be patronized. Just let me talk about it. No one has to do anything.

Yet with our children we always feel we have to be the answer man. We don't give them a chance to just talk it out. Maybe they just want to see how it sounds and get some feedback on a personal level. They are not always wanting to be told how to get out of a bind.

We've had a lot of experience communicating with our husband or wife. What are some of the good ways we've used? Let's speak and act those ways when we're talking with our children. Styles and topics of conversation may differ, but the principles of communication are the same.

What do we mean when we ask the children to listen to us? Of course we want them to listen, because it is one of the best ways we have of teaching them things that are important. All of us as children can remember our mother and father either saying very softly, but with great insistence, or shouting at us, "Will you listen to me!" All of us can say that we've done the same thing with our children. Are we just asking them to be obedient? That is what often comes across to our children. If they've done the task asked of them or stopped doing something we've forbidden them to do, then they feel they've listened. They may not have learned anything about us, they may have no empathy with us, they may have no responsiveness toward us. Instead, don't we really want them to listen to us as persons?

It isn't that obedience is not a good practice for children. There are things they must do and other things they must stop doing. But that has little to do with listening. If they respond because they really care for us and they want to show in this manner an awareness of who we are as persons, then that's listening. Obeying because they know they're going to get punished or because we're angry is not really listening to us.

We may equate listening with agreement. If the child comes around to our point of view or concedes our argumentation is better than his then we believe that he has listened to us. Of course that is far from true.

The chief reason our children don't listen to us is because we don't reveal ourselves. We don't want the children to see us in our weakness. We want to protect our image and keep our authority in front of them. We're afraid we're going to lose their respect if they know we are uncertain or have doubts.

Our children need to know that we are human. We come across to them as secure—so certain—so much in control. We don't seem to need them, and they know they need us very much—not just for the material things, but to be understood and cared about. One of our strengths should be to share with them our weaknesses. Then they can trust us. Then they can feel they have a part in our lives and can make a contribution to us.

So, before we even consider where they are in listening to us, we have to consider how much of ourselves we have given the children to listen to. Sometimes we excuse ourselves on the basis of, "They're too young to understand." "They're too insensitive." "They'll blab it all over the neighborhood." "They have enough problems of their own." But whatever the excuses, they really don't hold water. Using them, we run a terrible risk. If we don't reveal ourselves, not only will the child grow up a stranger in his own home, but he will grow up with strangers in his own home.

Do conversations with your children always have to come out your way?   *Your answer:*

Some of us are quite insistent that our children agree with us We may not use a heavy-handed type of force. Anger need

64

not be involved. Instead, we may give patient, careful explanations—with all the good will in the world and a tender love in our heart—to make sure that our children see the right way of going about things.

In a simple interchange at the dinner table or sitting around watching television together, do we have to pursue our viewpoint? Are we willing to change our mind? Are we ever willing to entertain doubts or to admit that maybe our son or daughter might be right? It's very difficult for them to believe that we are listening to them if even in simple discussion it always has to come out our way.

This doesn't come from any evil in us. It's just that we're used to looking on ourselves as being responsible for our children. From the goodness of our hearts we don't want them to make a mistake. Furthermore we have had more experience in being persuasive and in expressing a position than they have had. A lot of times our kids have good ideas, but they don't know how to express them.

Part of our listening to our children, therefore, can help them state what they want to say in an understandable way.

Wendy shared her projects—and we were proud.

When they obviously have something going on within them and it isn't being verbalized with any degree of clarity, then we can try to restate it for them, pointing out what might be a problem in their position.

What are the typical mistakes you make in listening to your children?

Your answer:

We seem to feel that we have to do all the talking when we are conversing with our children. It comes from our goodness. We're so convinced that we have to get our points across and that there are so many things that they have to learn that a conversation ends up all on our side. Oh, yes, we allow our children to tell us the things they've done, and we take a certain amount of interest in that. We may even allow them to express their opinions, but basically we're just waiting to tell them what we think they need to hear.

Another mistake we make is deciding that certain matters are above our children's heads or of no real interest to them. We don't listen when the youngsters bring them up or, if we do, we presume that the children have nothing to say, and just talk around them. The children then begin to discuss the topics only among themselves or with other people instead of with us. Implicitly we've told them that the subjects are forbidden as far as we are concerned, or that we're not interested in what they have to say.

We also tend to make the mistake of looking at what our children say and not at who they are. In any communication between persons, it's more important to discover the person than to discover the position! It's a challenge to discover what feelings are going on inside our children and to respond to them. It isn't that a child should have his way when he's upset,

66

or that we should back off from communicating something we think is important. However, in the normal interchange between parent and child, we shouldn't miss what's churning inside the child for the sake of getting our point across.

For example, do we ever allow our children to simply express their feelings without explaining them or without our trying to correct or change their feelings? Our children have the same needs that we have. Sometimes we want to just tell people how we feel. We don't expect them to do anything about it and we certainly don't want to be fixed up—we just want to be understood. Often our children just want to be understood.

The whole question of how to listen to feelings is terribly important. The best way to achieve rapport between persons is for them to have an interchange of feelings. We experience the responsiveness of another person when our feelings are in sync with his. Somtimes we take our children's feelings for granted and figure they will pass. We may have a certain amount of sympathy for their feelings. But because there are more important things on our minds, we don't want to get too involved with them. Other times when we think we are responding to the child's feelings, we're responding to our own. It may be because the child's feelings have been strong enough to cause similar or opposite feelings in us and we're reacting to them. We may vent our anger, or express our feelings of pity or tenderness—or what have you—but we're involved with ourselves, not the child.

How often do we tell our children that they shouldn't feel the way they're feeling? We're really asking them to control something that they are not able to control. Feelings come and go. Whether we feel up or down frequently depends upon the condition of our stomach or some external event that's taken place. For example, when we tell our children that they shouldn't feel nervous, we are training the child to hide the manifestations of nervousness. As he grows older he is apt to become very inward, with nervous feelings churning within him. A crippling of the personality can take place that is almost as bad as the physical crippling of Chinese girls 100 years ago when their feet were bound.

67

Another typical mistake that we make with our children is to be so busy doing all sorts of things for them that we never find time to listen. We're taking them here, there and everywhere. We're trying to make sure their talents are developed. We're seeing that they get their chores done around the house and their homework completed. It turns out that there's almost no time for us to be together with them—no time for us to be listening.

The first thing we can do to put our listening on a new track is to take a few moments and try to really listen to one of the children. We may discover marvelous things about that child!

Are you really looking for a relationship with your children?   *Your answer:*

We can easily snort out, "Yes, of course, we're looking for a relationship with our children. What else would we be looking for?" It's not that simple. There's no question about our sincerity in wanting the child to be happy, in wanting to do the right thing by the child, and wanting to provide everything that he needs to grow into a successful human being. But doing those things doesn't necessarily build a relationship.

We want the child to have fond memories of his childhood. We want to provide an atmosphere of protectiveness and security in which he can grow in wisdom and grace. All that's to the best, but we still may not be developing a relationship with that child. Developing a relationship with someone is entirely different from providing services for him.

One of the big difficulties is that we want our children to be dependent upon us. And they are, but it needs to be a two-way street. Sometimes we think they can't take independence —that they're not prepared for it. Actually what they can't take is the one-sidedness of a relationship that keeps them dependent. A good relationship is one in which I know and am known. I love and am loved. I experience you and you experience me. One of the deepest cries from our children's hearts is that they really want to know us. They often ask what we were like when we were little. What we were like when we dated and became engaged and married. What we were like in the early years of our marriage. They want to know everything about us, but more important they really want to know us. If we truly want a relationship with our children we have to listen to that sincere urgency in them to know us better. We can respond by sharing ourselves.

Our children also want to be wanted by us, not simply in terms of our wanting a baby or somebody to carry on our name or to be a comfort to us in our old age. They want us to want them as persons and have a full-fledged human relationship with them. They went to be a part of our hearts. They want to be involved in every aspect of our lives. That's what a love relationship truly is.

Do you assume your children are like all other children of their ages?

Your answer:

There is a set of physical and psychological characteristics that are common to five-year-olds, and another set of characteristics common to 10-year-olds, etc. It's a simple process to draw the conclusion that our three-year-old should be like other three-year-olds and our teenager should be like other

"Mom and I made it for you, Daddy."

teenagers. Consequently we read up on the different stages of growth. When we recognize in our children some of the characteristics we've read about indicating that they are passing through certain stages, we are inclined to ascribe all the other characteristics to them. The result is that we treat our children as typical cases. While we're talking to Jimmy or Susie, we're talking to this composite type of person we've read about. Anything Jimmy or Susie does or says that is different from the typical we suppress in our consciousness. We highlight just those characteristics that reinforce our convictions that Jimmy is a typical three-year-old and Susie is a typical teen.

We do this because it's more simple to cope with someone who is typical than with someone who is different. We can get a set of answers that are universally applicable and not have to go through the complicated struggle of trying to understand a person on an individual basis. But when we take the easy way, we don't get through to the personality of our child.

Do you assume you know exactly what your children will say?

Your answer:

An observant mother or father can frequently read the reactions their children are going to have. But because we are convinced that we know the kind of persons our children are, we are tempted into a variety of negative actions.

We may know that the child is quick or mercurial and has a tendency to be moody, or is very insightful, or has a quick temper. In order to correct an overreaction or modify what we're convinced is a tendency in him, we step in right away in any circumstances that might stimulate that type of response and complete his sentences for him. Our behavior is a self-fulfilling prophecy because we teach the child by our response what we expect from him or her.

Assumptions are always the enemy of relationship. We decide in our own minds what we can reasonably expect in any given circumstance from the person with whom we are dealing. Then we are excused from paying any attention to what the other person is saying. It's a difficult position for a child to be in because he has to compete with what we have in our mind about him. He's always trying to live up to—or to correct—what we assume we know about him.

Another assumption that hinders relationships is to believe that "we've heard that song before." We assume that we know exactly where our child is in his development because our older children have gone through it before. Or, we've heard the child talk about a topic in such and such a way before, so we're convinced in our own mind that we know exactly what will follow and we only half listen.

There are also subjects to which we are closed because we've already talked about them to the child and he was rigid in his views or held a position that we thought was unreasonable. We really don't want to get into a discussion again, because we feel there's no possibility of getting anywhere and we don't want to play ring around the rosey. Of course, then we are as stubborn as we think they are.

If we think the child has been influenced by somebody else, an older brother or sister, or a friend, we hear what that person is saying in this child's words, and assume the child's conclusion when he has just begun to talk.

Sometimes we don't listen to our children because we don't want to respond affirmatively to the request that the child is making. It may be concerning hours or amount of allowance or companionship or whatever. We assume that if we listen we might have to change our position. But real listening concerns itself strictly and solely with being aware of the other person. It still leaves us free to say no. Even if something is very important to a child, he can take a difference of opinion or a denial if he feels that he's been listened to. Expecting heavy pressure doesn't excuse us from listening to the person behind the statements.

There is a big defect in the parent-child relationship when it's all do's and don'ts or a series of requests granted or denied. Communication of personhood is not taking place. We have to go deeper to find out what feelings are inside that child.

One day I heard Betty interrupt her telephone conversation to ask her dad if she could go to a friend's house. Ted felt it was probably better for her not to go because Grandma might stop over. Betty said into the phone indignantly, "My dad won't let me!" Ted was sorry he had answered rather quickly and asked Betty if she really wanted to go. "No," she grinned. Why had she asked her dad? Betty acknowledged that she needed his no and appreciated it! She had inserted the antagonism to parallel the way her friend talked about parents.

We'll probably be surprised with what we find out when, like Ted, we go behind what the child is saying and get to his feelings. It can happen when we have an inkling that a conversation is not going to go well—when the child has been disobedient or is becoming defiant. Our temptation is to turn off the child by insisting upon our authority. But this is a time when we should be listening to him more intently than ever.

Sometimes our difficulty in listening comes from painful past experiences. When we get close to a similar situation, we assume that we're going to end up hurting again, so we become arbitrary. Actually, this is a time for us not to insist upon our position, much less our authority. We need to try to talk out what's going on inside of us—to let the child in on our confusion, consternation, anger or loneliness that we're experiencing. Then the child can talk on a personal level and reveal himself. Maybe then we can get through some of the barriers that exist.

How do you respond to what your children say?   *Your answer:*

74

Frequently it's easier to be patient, understanding and responsive to another person's children than to our own. With them, we can maintain objectivity. We are emotionally involved with our own children. When they make statements or do things that irritate us we tend to over-react.

Very often we act in the same childish way we resent in them. We often don't even listen to them because of some little incident to which we shouldn't pay any attention at all.

It's one thing to reject another person's position on a point; it's another thing to reject the person. We get so upset by what our children say to us that we sometimes forget they are our children. We get involved in straightening them out instead of loving them out. We would be further ahead by loving them than by constantly correcting them.

Do you pay attention to your children's body language?

Your answer:

We're good at reading body language when it comes to our children's well-being. We have a special eye that looks for a touch of pallor, circles under the eyes, a drooping head, or dragging feet. We know a child is feeling under the weather even before he does.

We would do well to be as astute and sensitive to body language when our children are trying to talk to us! We can be aware of their nervousness or their shyness, their false bravado or brashness, so that we will respond with sympathy. We know the telltale signs when something is serious within them, and yet, all too often, we're too busy working, too occupied in getting our point across, or too upset by what they've just said to really take the signals to heart. We see, without seeing, the squeezing of the nails into the palms of the hands, the shifting of the feet, the hanging head, the averted eyes, or the earnestness on the face.

Sometimes we notice a different tone of voice or a special look on the face. That's the time for us to switch gears, to get off the topic with which we're concerned, and to get onto the child. What he says in ram-rod defiance may be from a conviction within himself that he is not being listened to. What he speaks in anger may really be frustration. Statements that are made with self-confidence and sweeping conviction could be a cry for help and understanding. If we just hear words, we're not going to listen to persons. Reading our children's body language will help us know them.

When you are talking with your children, do you look into their eyes?   *Your answer:*

When we're talking to a person, we often look over his shoulder, busy ourselves doing other things, or look into his face generally, but not into his eyes. We will listen better—and let our children know we are really listening to them—if we look into their eyes, gently encouraging them. We can see into the person of the child through his eyes and get not only words, but a real sense of his being.

Maybe your son was telling you something confusing about school and you were getting concerned—and then you saw the mischief in his eyes and knew he was teasing. Or, you were upset with your daughter and saw her stubbornness and heard the anger in her voice. Then you glimpsed the hurt in her eyes, and it changed your whole approach.

"He's special, Dad, like you are to Mom."

The old American battle cry of "don't fire until you see the whites of their eyes" is also true with our children!

Do you touch your children when you are talking seriously with them?   *Your answer:*

Touching is an important part of non-verbal communication and an expression of personal involvement. When there's meaningful communication going on between people they need to be touching one another.

In any family, touching usually gets reduced to certain ritualistic times. We hug and kiss one another when we come and go, say goodnight, when we've received a present, or when something special happens to us.

Actually, in order for us to become personal with one another it has to be touched out of us. We need the security, the reassurance of the other person's hands on us to know that we are being accepted, that we are being understood. This is especially important for children.

As long as we're touching our children we're going to be more responsive to them. We're going to be more absorbed in the child, more in contact with him. The ability to touch is a gift from the Lord, and our hands can be truly loving. We should use them much more with our children than we do. We constantly touch our children when they are little, and we know how important it is. It is good for both us and the children. However, as they grow older, we tend to hold back. We touch them less and less. We need to realize that we are not going to be "in touch" with our children unless we are touching them. Isn't it easier to be aware of someone and know what is going on inside him if we're in physical contact?

Touching is a gentle way of communicating our presence, especially our listening presence. Sometimes the best way to listen is through our fingertips rather than through our ears. We can learn so much of where a child is within himself by picking the tot up in our arms or by putting our arms around our son's or daughter's shoulders. Skin to skin is a very important aspect of our listening apparatus. There's a sensitivity and a responsiveness that comes about in us when we're touching.

Barry made me realize that. He was one of the nicest boys in my class. He was always prepared, paid attention in school, was eager to learn. One day he didn't have his assignment and I told him to stay after class. He came, but told me calmly he wasn't going to stay. I was shocked and blurted out, "You just think you're not. For your punishment, write a composition on one of the inventors we studied last week." He said no and started to leave. I reached out for him not, I must confess, with any idea of communication, but simply to get his attention. I felt his muscles stiff as a board. I knew now that I would hurt that fine boy if I insisted on the extra assignment. He couldn't talk it out now—he was too uptight—so I said, "Hey, Barry, why don't you go and talk to me when you feel like it." The next Monday he came in after class with compositions written on two inventors! He explained that he had honestly forgotten the original assignment and was so embarrassed in front of the class that he just wasn't himself. He was grateful I hadn't pushed him to the wall!

We shouldn't always leave our touching to the times when we're spontaneously moved or when someone's been physically hurt or emotionally upset. We should be touching our children in normal circumstances. It is amazing to discover how much we learn from our children, both verbally and non-verbally, when we come in bodily contact with them.

Touching is serious and important. It can be just a brushing against the child, a squeeze on the arm, a pat on the head, or just a simple touch on the hand. But we let the child know that we're there, that we care, and that we're ready to listen to him.

We may try to excuse ourselves by saying, "Well, we're just

"It's a big secret, Daddy—just for you and Mom."

not the touching type." The reason why we're not the touching type is that we aren't touching. There's a space between us and other people. We're keeping our distance—or they are. The only way people become the touching type is by touching.

Touching our children tenderizes us, makes us conscious of our relationship with them and willing to respond to them as persons. Touching is a beautiful thing.

Do you let your children touch you?
Your answer:

Children are natural touchers. They want to touch everything with which they come in contact. When a parent takes a child someplace, he says over and over, "Don't touch that!"

Our children, by natural inclination, have a real desire to touch us. We may be among those people who don't feel like being touched. Sometimes our not wanting our children to touch us is very conscious and explicit. We shake them off and tell them, "Don't try to get around me," or, "Just stand over there so I can talk to you." Or if we don't say anything, we keep ourselves moving about and our hands busy so that there's very little opportunity for them to touch us.

But children need the assurance of having our attention by taking hold of us. Some things they want to say can only come out if they're hanging on. They can only be assured of our listening to them if they have our physical as well as our mental attention. It's easier for them to trust us when they're feeling us. It's easier for them to listen and be responsive.

If we think that our children aren't very good listeners or that they don't pay much attention to us, then we have to examine how much we let them touch us. If we discover that there is very little touching, then the solution is within us!

**Do you listen more
to other people
than to your children?**   *Your answer:*

It's easy to fall into the trap of listening to others rather than to our own children. It isn't that we should not seek advice. After all, our parents gained a lot of experience over the years in raising us, and we would be foolish to overlook it. Too, the mothers and fathers in the neighborhood are working hard at raising their children. They are experiencing many of the same dilemmas we are in trying to communicate with their children. Furthermore, there are a lot of good books sold on child psychology and child rearing.

However, there is a danger that we don't listen to our children at all. Many times we allow a teacher or some other adult to tell us what our child is like rather than allowing our child to tell us what he is like. And that's just it. To communicate with our children we need to listen to them!

**Do you listen to
your children only
enough to solve the
immediate problem?**   *Your answer:*

If we look on life as a series of problems, then solving a problem makes us feel that everything's all right.

Actually a child is like any other human being. What that

child needs more than anything else is human understanding, and that's not accomplished by a surface solution or by merely giving him the right answers to his questions of the moment. That child needs to know if we are involved with him.

There is a difference between our telling our daughter all the right reasons for not letting her go to a certain place and our really feeling with her about being left out.

It's often easy for us to take our children's disappointments in stride. They don't always get to us where we live. We don't always get involved emotionally.

It's like a woman's no concerning intimacies before and after marriage. The no is the same both times, but before marriage it hurts her—she cares about all his feelings. After marriage, it's not so hard for her to say no. She may feel a certain sympathy for him, but the situation is different. In both cases there is physical frustration for the husband, but in the second case he also feels personal rejection. That's where the real pain is.

With our children we also have to say no sometimes, but if we understand how they feel, and care about their disappointment, it's easier for them to accept the refusal. They feel our involvement.

What makes it difficult for you to listen to your children?   *Your answer:*

Normal everyday occurrences provide a lot of barriers to communication. We're very busy people. There are so many things that have to be done! There's a house to be cleaned and meals to be prepared, there's a living to be earned, there are books to be read. We have duties in our parish or neighborhood. We have responsibilities to one another and to our parents. Sometimes we feel torn in 17 different directions.

Our moods are another problem. We're not always in the best possible shape on any given day or for every moment of every day. There are times when we're upset because of some personal thing that's going on inside of us, or something that somebody said, or a worrisome event that's coming up. We're not always prepared to listen.

Often our children are not sensitive to what is going on—understandably—and they come at us in ways that make it extremely difficult to listen. They come with a flood of requests, a stubborn insistence to pursue their point, or with an impatience in their voices that tends to trigger a response of impatience in us.

Because there are relatively few occasions when we can really get ourselves up to listen well, we better seize those occasions, plan them out ahead of time. We have to look within ourselves and unclutter our minds when we're with our children. We need to ask ourselves, "How can I be more myself with the children? How can I let them be more themselves with me?"

First, we can let them know that we're going to give them a special time—a time that's going to be just for them, and we're going to give them our full selves. This is not the only time of day that they can talk to us, but at this special time we're going to be completely at their disposal. It doesn't have to be a long period of time, but during those moments we'll listen! We, as well as the children, will know that time is there. Usually when something special or important to us is going to happen, we savor the moment well ahead of time, think about it, plan for it. If our communication with our children is important to us, we'll feel the same way.

One of our biggest barriers to preparing to talk with our children is that we really don't consider it to be all that important. We think we know pretty much what they're going to talk about, and we know what our answers are going to be. We think that's all there is to it. We have to revise that position and recognize that the children are important, that they

Life is a puzzle too.

have many more things on their minds than we have yet discerned, and that more important than any of the answers we give them is our relationship with them.

Every mother knows what after 3 o'clock on a school afternoon is like. It's a hectic time of quick hugs and kisses, loud chatter and peanut butter and jelly sandwiches. Liz, a good mother who has made a Marriage Encounter weekend with us, told me that many times it was easier for her to just keep half an ear cocked rather than to really listen to the children after school. It seemed to her as though they just talked about routine details. One day she had been jarred when Tim threw his sandwich into the sink and cried, "Mom, you're really not listening to me—you're just pretending to!" He was dead right. Liz didn't know what he or his two sisters had been talking about. Later, she found out. Tim had missed only one arithmetic problem out of 75 in a test that day! (He'd been having a terrible time with math.) The breakthrough had come, and Liz had missed it. She said it took her some days of listening to convince Tim that she really did care.

It's also difficult to listen to our children when they bring up topics we don't want to talk about. We may feel we don't have the answers, or that we do but they are too complicated.

Maybe we really don't know when we shut down our mental listening apparatus. We're going to have to ask our children to tell us when they find it hardest to communicate with us. That can be a very humbling experience—but a tremendous one—as the children realize we care about listening to them. We can also ask them when they feel most listened to, and how we act at those times. That way we will discover some of our good points! We can then consciously become better listeners—to the mutual profit of both ourselves and our children.

When you don't listen to your children, what happens to your relationship with them?

Your answer:

Listening to our children opens doors; not listening to our children closes—even locks—doors. When we don't listen, the children tend to talk at us. They begin to clam up. A barrier grows between us. There's a whole area of our lives in which we're not experiencing each other, and that's a great loss for both the parents and the children. It's true that children should have other relationships; they should ask questions and seek advice of other people. But the relationship with their parents is a special one, and the children should feel perfectly free to be their full selves with their mother and father. If being listened to is not a real aspect of the relationship, then that relationship is hurting.

Jackie is as sincere and as good a wife as you would ever hope to find. Mac, her husband, is solid and true—all 6'6" of him! I enjoy them and their children very much. Whenever their 14-year-old Judy has a question, a worry, she comes to me and asks my advice. I know that it's good for Judy to have adult family friends to talk to, but she and Mac and Jackie are missing out on so much in each other! I've told Judy that, but she is convinced that her folks won't understand her questions about boys, sex, church—or talk with her of what life is all about. She just tells them what she thinks they want to know. That's heartbreaking.

How does your relation-   *Your answer:*
ship with your spouse
affect listening
to your children?

When our relationship with our husband or wife is uneasy, difficult or distant we listen to the children differently than when everything is fine. As a matter of fact, we may feel closer than ever to the children in those unpleasant circumstances. We may be unusually open and caring with them. Actually we're looking to receive from our children what we should be receiving from our husband or wife.

On the other hand, when there's an uncomfortable atmosphere between us, we tend to see in the children the things we dislike in our spouse. Because we can't correct them in our spouse, we nag at the children. We want to make sure our children don't act that way! So, we are harsher in our reaction to the child at those times than when our relationship is going smoothly.

When the relationship between husband and wife is solid and loving, it overflows to the children. There's nothing better than that!

What is the cumulative effect of listening?

Your answer:

Out of a listening relationship comes trust. Children in such an environment believe they are accepted as persons regardless of the mistakes they make or how inadequately they express themselves. This is the most wonderful experience that any human being can have, and it's the best preparation for becoming a loving person.

The greatest legacy parents can leave their children is for them to say in the years to come, "When I was growing up, I was really listened to." That's more important than all the education or all the money in the world. The proudest boast that any parent can make of himself is, "I really listened to my children." Listening makes more of a difference in the happiness level and the fullness of life for our children than any other experience they can have.

YOUR CHILDREN ARE A UNIQUE REPLAY OF YOU IN YOUR COUPLENESS.

3

REPLAYS

Who are your children?   *Your answer:*

Parents love to describe their children. We never tire of telling what our sons and daughters have done or said, and we
sometimes add, "—he's just like his dad," or "—she's just like
her mother." In many ways our children are replays of us. Do
we see it that way? Or when we're asked who our children
are, do we say, "Well, there's Janie who is 14, and Timmy
who is 8, and Tony who is 3."

That doesn't explain *who* they are, does it? No, of course
not. Do we explain them any better if we give their heights,
color of hair and eyes, the marks they get in school, their
hobbies, their interests, the particular talents they have, or

even the qualities that are special to them? It is true that we're describing persons, but the descriptions are not unique. Something is missing.

The question still remains, "Who are your children?" It's the *your* that is the key to the question. "Who are *your* children?" Identification is involved. They have their own personhood and their own personalities, but they are not isolated entities. They are not separate from *you*.

Do you really feel they are yours just because of a physical process, because a birth certificate says so, or because you adopted them and have assumed the responsibility to take care of them until they're old enough? In other words, is the "your" just something genetic and legal? Is their identity with you only dependent upon the fact that there was a moment of conception and nine months of pregnancy? It seems for the most part that that's the view of both parents and children.

Children recognize that they got their start in life from this man and woman whom they call mother and father and that they owe them a tremendous debt of gratitude for all the sacrifices and all the gifts of love poured out over the years. But usually they don't see their real personal identity as coming from the parents. Oh, they know that there are genetic qualities in them, that their strength of body and mind comes from their parents. But they don't really connect the fullness of their personhood with their parents. For example, their soul is looked on as a separate entity, so they feel they have an existence separate from their parents. This is not limited to children. It's only part of the picture. Parents and children are not totally separate entities. Your children are not your children without you. They are a complex replay of *you* in your coupleness.

Does "your" mean just you, yourself?   *Your answer:*

94

When we talk about "your" children, is "your" singular or plural in your mind? In other words, do you think about yourself pretty much as one individual in relationship with your children? It's easy for us to do so. It's especially easy for women, because they're the ones that have borne the children for nine months, given birth to them, and usually spent the most time with them. Motherhood becomes an overriding focus. The mother's concentration is on the relationship with her child. Of course she is aware that there was a father involved and that she couldn't have had the child without his contribution. Furthermore, she's very glad for her husband's support in raising the children. She appreciates him even more if there's real cooperation and involvement, if they can get together in responding to the children's needs. That's exactly what parenthood is—a cooperative effort of two people who have a single stake in this one person, their child.

It is important for us to face the reality that children never have a single parent regardless of what the external circumstances may be. Children are always expressive of a duality.

**When did your
children begin?**

Your answer:

A child's physical being begins at the moment of conception, but in another way, that spot in time was a culmination rather than a beginning.

It's common to remark that a child was a gleam in the father's eye, but behind that teasing there's a deep reality. Our children are a crowning touch of our relationship. It is our awareness of one another and responsiveness to one another that creates a desire in us to have a living expression of our love.

Actually it's only when our love is complete that we can commit ourselves to having a child by one another. A child is a seal to our love. Having a child expresses our trust in one another and says that our relationship is not a passing fancy, that we're involved in a relationship that's enduring and fully open.

A child in his full identity is a statement about our relationship with one another. Our willingness to take the risk of creating a life that is ours can only come about when we have a real desire to have a complete love with our spouse. So our children speak to us. They show forth our love for one another and our commitment to one another better than anything else.

One of the great joys in our life as a couple comes when we realize our oneness in our child. Our love is so special that it cannot just be called love; it must have a specific name that testifies to its uniqueness. We must call our love Johnny or Jimmy or Mary. That love of ours is so vital that we cannot keep it to ourselves, we must speak it to the world. So our children are not a creation of our physical activity so much as they are a creation of our personal relationship.

Before conception takes place it is impossible to think of the child without thinking of our spouse. In our minds our children are conceived in terms of our awareness of the other person and what that other person means to us. It's not just a child we want, it's *his* child, it's *her* child, that we want to bring to life. As the children come along, we get absorbed in them and in our responsibilities. We lose sight of what we were so clear-minded about in the very beginning—that the reality of each child is important because of the person we love. Instead we tend to become custodial: Our relationship with our children becomes one of taking care of daily needs, doing the right things by them and preparing them for later life. In the beginning the whole notion of having children was to do something for our spouse.

What happens when the children are center stage?   *Your answer:*

When we as parents focus our attention on the children, we're not being as selfless as we think. Rather, parenthood becomes a self-conscious, self-centered experience, and not out of any badness. But there is a problem. We judge how we are doing as parents strictly by looking at the effect on the child. If we don't do the right thing by our children we're afraid that we're going to be failures, that we're going to be rejected by them. Actually what we should be doing is looking at the effect on our spouse!

I remember a lovely family of a boy I was teaching. Danny was a fine kid, but he was driving his father up the wall because he just wouldn't study. Mike, his dad, desperately wanted his boy to have a better life than his as a bus driver. He didn't want him to have to go out at 5 o'clock every morning and drive in downpours, blizzards and heat waves.

More and more, his attention focused on how Danny did in school. As soon as Mike came home, he checked up on Danny. Many a night he and Margaret talked about what to do. Nothing seemed to work. Danny kept promising he'd do better, but when he'd go to his room to do his homework, he'd end up reading a sports magazine or rearranging the pennants on his wall.

Then Margaret got sick. Mike didn't talk about Danny because he didn't want to add to her burdens. He began to spend more time just being with her, and they began to talk about themselves. Margaret improved. Mike found himself thinking less and less about Danny's future and more and more about how lucky he was to have Margaret. He began to laugh more, and he found coming home more pleasant.

Danny, too, began to relax. He saw his father's tenderness and goodness with his mother. Before he had only seen his dad acting as a policeman. Mike began to sense some of Margaret's gentle, calm nature in Danny, and he loved him for it.

One day Mike found Danny's report card with a note to him saying, "I love you, Dad, because you love Mom." He had passed everything and even had one "A." Mike realized he hadn't thought about Danny's homework, much less gotten on his back about it for some time! He'd been absorbed in Margaret—that had solved the problem.

"Squash me some more!"

Our whole relationship with our children is going to be different if we focus on our spouse rather than on our children. Sometimes we think that the more attention we pay directly to our children, the more they're going to feel loved and appreciated. Actually the more absorbed that we are with one another, and the more the children continue to get their meaning from our relationship with one another, the more life they're going to have.

It's not that children are not important in themselves and that they don't have lives of their own. But they're most enriched when they're loved because of our love for one another.

When we face directly into our children our relationship may be in terms of what we're going to get out of it. It's true that we all find a great deal of satisfaction, self-fulfillment and purpose to life because we're a father or a mother. It memorializes us. We know our name will not die with us. We know that we will have grandchildren; that there will be somebody to take care of us in old age; and that there are ones dependent on us, giving us a sense of worth.

These benefits can lead us to do all sorts of good things for our children, and the children may turn out very well. But if we are chiefly motivated by them, then we're missing the true greatness of our calling. We are to be involved first and foremost with our spouse. Otherwise, each is dealing with his children, personally and privately, and the children are half orphans. They are deprived. The greatest thing that can happen to children is for them to be able to say not simply that they are loved, but that they are loved through their parents' love for each other. A child can never feel alienated or rejected or burdensome when the whole thrust of our relationship with him is in terms of who we are to our spouse.

Frank seemed to be one of those kids who never had a care in the world or a thought in his head. But he came to see me one evening and said he was dropping out of school. He felt the tuition was too much of a sacrifice for his parents. He was going to quit and get a job and help out at home. I used all the standard arguments, but nothing got to him.

Soon afterwards his parents came to see me, all upset. They were such good people. They wanted what was best for Frank. It suddenly struck me what an awful burden that was for Frank! Their whole life was tied up in him. Every day that poor kid must have felt he was on the foul line of the championship game with 2 shots and his team down by one.

"Why did you two get married?" I asked them. "Did you get married for Frank's sake?"

"Well, we hoped to have kids."

"Sure, but you got married to love one another. The best way to love Frank is to love one another. That's the way he got his start in life and that's what he needs most of all now!"

A question that all children ask is, "How did I come to be, why do I exist, what is my purpose in life?" They are not asking simply in terms of what they're going to do with their lives or how they're going to have some kind of significant impact on this world. They want to know what the purpose was right from the beginning and what it is in their very existence right at this moment. If the answer is, "We wanted you because we mean so much to one another. And we continue to want you for that very same reason," then they have a magnificence of purpose that is incomparable.

When the child is constantly being responded to in terms of our responsiveness to one another—our relationship—he

100

doesn't have to make it on his own; he's already got it made. And our benefit is great.

Most boys and girls I know talk about their parents individually, or in terms of what they do or don't do for them. Sam always talked about his folks in terms of their relationship with one another, and he didn't hesitate to say, "My mom and dad neck every night on the couch." He added, "They tease each other a lot." Sam's eyes lit up and his whole body came alive. "They have so much fun. Mom can never resist Dad when he puts his arms around her, and Dad just loves it when Mom sweet-talks him. They always have little surprises for each other, and they really understand each other. I'm the luckiest guy in the world!"

If the whole environment in which we as a couple face into our children is one in which we're really expressing our love to one another, then we have the security of our faithfulness to one another and our total commitment to one another to carry us through any rough times.

Another way of saying this whole thing is that the child isn't so much to be hugged by his mother and his father as to be squeezed between them hugging one another. Then the child is enveloped in love—totally surrounded by love.

There is no fear in this type of relationship that the child is going to be ignored, taken advantage of, or even to be less well taken care of. As a matter of fact, there is no way that the child could be more tenderly and beautifully treated. And any selfishness or egoism we might have slips away when a child is not absorbing all our attention but is in on this special love of ours.

Billy is a very restless little boy. He's into everything and he's very demanding of attention. Marriage Encounter couple Bart and Fran agree that he, more than their other children, seems to need more of their time and attention. He's always saying, "Mommy, look at this." "Daddy, play with me." Bart told me, "There is one time when he's the quietest, most restful child you'd ever want to meet. That's at those moments when Fran and I are sitting side by side holding hands or with our arms around each other. Billy sits at our feet or curls

101

up on our lap. He doesn't say a word or move a muscle. He just wants to be part of us."

When is parenting finished?   *Your answer:*

If our focus is on a direct relationship with the children, then parenting ends as soon as the children leave home. We feel our children don't need us anymore. We ask, "What's going to happen? We just have one another, so what are we ever going to do?"

Parenthood is to give life, and it never ends. It's not something that is accomplished by a certain time. The call to parenthood is a call to integrate our children into our continuing and ever-deepening love for one another. That's what brought them into being in the first place. That's what creates their identity. So whether our children are zygotes or full-fledged men and women of 30, or 40 or 50 years old, we still have the call to bring them to life. It's not a question of a job assignment that has a cut-off date. Parenthood is not a job. There are jobs and tasks connected with parenthood, but that's not what defines parenthood. Actually all those tasks could be performed very well and very lovingly by those who have no relationship whatsoever to the children, just as a man and woman can do married things for one another without being married. It's a couple's commitment to be totally involved with one another that says they are married. In parenthood, it's bringing our children constantly to new life by our love for one another that says we are parents. If our love for one another doesn't increase, then we stunt our children's lives. If we didn't feed them properly, or take proper medical care of them, their physical lives would be ruined or impeded.

Their lives as persons also need constant nourishment and embellishment, and that is only accomplished by our awareness that they are an extension of us. What we do for one another we're really doing for them. Just as a man doesn't make a distinction between himself and his body, so a parent can't make a distinction between the relationship with the children and the relationship with his spouse.

Maureen is a great mother. She really works at it. Her kids are always neat and clean, do well in school, all the other kids love to go to her house—she loves having her children's friends around. She plays with her children, tucks them in at night, reads stories to them, gets up during the night to get them a glass of water or hold them close if they are having a nightmare. If there were a contest in our parish for the most wonderful mother, Maureen would be a finalist. But the award would have to be for most wonderful unwed mother, even though she and Kevin had a beautiful church ceremony, 11 years ago.

Actually, Kevin is just as good a father as she is a mother. Their kids are lucky, and they'll be even luckier if Kevin and Maureen ever decide to be really married. Right now all their kids ever see are two wonderful people who have taken them on as a community project.

On their 12th wedding anniversary when Maureen brought out their wedding album and photographs of their dating days, the children were thunderstruck. They couldn't believe their folks had ever been young and happy with eyes only for each other. After that, the pictures were left out in plain sight, and other past experiences came to light.

Maureen and Kevin took another look at each other. They realized they were giving so much of their time and attention to their children, they weren't giving them what they most had to give—their love for one another. "You know, Kevin," said Maureen, "as far as our kids are concerned, we could be brother and sister raising them. Let's give our marriage priority and let our children know we love one another."

Now some parents want to always control their children. Other parents relax and breathe a sigh of relief thinking their job will be done once their children reach a certain age. Both miss the best part of what parenthood is about. Being a parent is far too cosmic and far too significant for it ever to be static or accomplished. It's organic, constantly being accomplished, so in the true sense of the term a person is never a parent, he is always becoming a parent.

How important is it to let your children know they are irreplaceable?

Your answer:

If we're just one of hundreds of millions then it's hard for us to see how we have any particular value. That's why it's easy for people to throw their lives away on drugs or promiscuity or a careless seeking after pleasure. They really don't think that it makes any difference to anyone.

If our children know they are the living, breathing statement of the love that we have for each other, they are unique individuals. Consequently they can never be replaced. They have a value that is absolutely precious and totally priceless.

Most of us look on ourselves as nothing special, and we don't see that we have much goodness in us. There's a lot of self-rejection in almost all of us. We can change that for our children. In the reality of their being loved, as a flesh-and-blood speaking out of a husband's and wife's love for each other, then self-rejection becomes an impossibility. Each child can look on himself as a gift that the husband and wife gave to one another—a very precious gift that's treated with particular care and concern and tenderness.

Nothing else that a husband and wife can do for one another compares with the gift of a child. In that very creation the two will be forever entwined. Even if they were to desert

Let's let the children know we love each other.

one another, the remnants of what they once meant to each other would always exist in their children.

Actually, our relationship with one another gives our children their identity. Being the expression of our love gives them their dignity, their worth and their value to themselves. They are not going to look on themselves as just another pebble on the beach. They're going to recognize that they're special and have a particular value in life that is absolutely irreplaceable.

Debbie is a "golden girl." Everybody likes her. She has confidence in herself and loves life. She knows her parents love each other. They are always together, always talking to one another. Debbie loves the fact that they have so much fun with one another and still hold hands even after being married 19 years.

Many youngsters whom I know are sad, aimless, lonely. It really hurts me.

I try to give them a sense of purpose, so they will feel they have a contribution to make. But it's hard to persuade them of that when they don't think they're anything special. I've tried everything to give boys and girls a sense of uniqueness. Oh, yes, they admit there is no one exactly like them. But that's true of fingerprints.

I know of no cure for this awful predicament other than giving them the kind of love we're talking about. I've never met boys or girls with identity problems who were loved through their parents loving each other and showing it.

How do you treat your children when they become adults?   *Your answer:*

Many couples tend to treat their grown children as used-to-be's. They act toward their sons and daughters as people who "used to be" their children. Oh, they know they still have some kind of a continuing relationship with them, and there are ties that bind them together. But now they feel that the children exist on their own and have their own lives to live, that they are separate from their parents—not just in the location sense, or in terms of having their own families, but in the sense of having a completely different life. However, the only life they really still have is an extension of their parents. Whatever they are and whatever their relationships with other people, they are the continuing expression of the relationship that brought them into being in the first place. That relationship can continue to give them significance and value.

We have a very narrow and restricted view of what life is. We should look on life as we look on air; as soon as we get some, we need more. So what parents have to provide is an atmosphere in which the children can breathe them in and out continuously. Parenthood continues to the last breath of one's life.

Kate, a dear 81-year-old lady I know, finds herself always welcome in her son's home. Sol and Sue love to have her babysit, of course, and they enjoy her loaves of Irish soda bread, but most of all they appreciate what she does for their relationship. She talks about Sol's dad and what he and she meant to one another.

Sol learns more about himself and his qualities as he learns more about his father's and mother's love, and he pays more attention to Sue. Although his dad has been dead for a number of years, he and Kate are still giving Sol life.

Yes, parents of a 45-year-old son and a 52-year-old daughter have just as much responsibility and just as much opportunity to give them life as they did at the moment of their conception. This obviously has nothing to do with running their lives or making the decisions for them in their marriages. It does have a lot to do with how much we allow them to taste and to touch our love for one another. But when we put our spouse second and focus on our children, trying to attract and absorb their attention, we fall into the smother-love trap. The attention we're angling for from our grown-up children rightfully belongs to their husbands or wives or children. We only do it when we don't have a deep and continuing relationship with our own husband or wife.

It is sad to see grandparents who just don't seem to have any purpose in their relationship other than convenience. What they are probably doing is the same thing they did with their own children. They used to put all their energy and attention directly on their children. Now, they're putting all their emphasis on the grandchildren. There's a double bypass. In the raising of their children, they bypassed their relationship with one another. Now they're bypassing that and their relationship with their children. They believe their children have no more need for them. They sometimes feel this way even when the relationship between parents and children is a good one. But they need to realize they're not finished, they've not served their purpose, that there's more they can give their children than helping them out financially or helping them fix up the house or giving some things to the grandchildren or helping to babysit.

They can continue to give life to the children by exposing them to their love for one another.

So whether the children are two years old or forty-two, the parents should look on them as an expression of their husband/wife relationship. In that way, the life-giving process is never ended. It's an ongoing one, and the children constantly become more assured as they become aware of who they really are.

**Do you see your
children as the two
of you in one flesh?**   *Your answer:*

One of the most beautiful expressions dealing with marriage is, "And the two shall be one flesh." The most obvious application of that is the sexual experience, but it means much more than that. The unity of a husband and wife is to be in mind and heart and affection as well as in body. The vocation of marriage is a call to live, not separate lives anymore, but a combined life. We are to gradually integrate ourselves into one another to become a real union of persons.

This is not easy, because all of us, in all probability, have a background of being treated as individuals instead of as expressions of a relationship. Consequently we have to reverse the pattern that has been deeply ingrained within us. It's a long process.

Sometimes it seems so difficult that we don't even consider that the "oneness" relationship can exist. We abandon any efforts to achieve it and settle for just getting along with one another. However, if we look at the physical dimensions, we can be aware of some of the possibilities. Have you ever seen an older couple who look alike physically? It is one of the phenomena of marriage that a couple who have been married 50 or 60 years have grown to look alike physically. If you were to see their wedding pictures, you'd never have believed they could look alike. But there's really no magic to it. Part of it is caused by old-age shrinkage, but much of it is caused by their having taken on each other's frown and smile lines. Their faces have become a common face. If this is true of the body, it is also true of the soul.

The physical look-alikeness is an indication that soul-alikeness has taken place. The face is an indication of the type of life they have lived together—the kind of couple that they have become. They have modified each other, and they have taken on each other's good points and qualities and rubbed off some of the rough edges that were there when they began their marriage. All this is very real and very beautiful. However, the truest and most total expression of the two of us in one flesh is our children. That is certainly beyond dispute physically. After all, half of their chromosomes come from each of us. We notice the physical similarities from the beginning. Isn't that one of the things we do right in the hospital nursery? We point out that the baby looks like his mother or father or his nose comes from his father's side of the family and his eyes from his mother's side.

As the child is growing up we recognize certain physical characteristics as being expressive of us or our spouse. Maybe he's delicately boned or broad-shouldered, light in complexion or dark. The older the child gets, the more similarities we notice.

More is involved than just the externals. The child's intelligence comes from us, and his coordination and personality qualities—patience, stick-to-itiveness, volatility, studiousness, sensitivity, concern for others, generosity, or a willingness to be self-sacrificing.

We often consider the miracle of birth. Unfortunately we limit the birth to the moment the child physically appears in this world. Actually birth is more than that, and it is constantly taking place. It's a miracle to have the child born of our love again and again and again!

At any given moment in the child's life he or she is a summary of our love relationship for one another. The child is a very good barometer of where we are standing with one another. He is more confident, more relaxed and more at ease when things are smooth between us than when they are not.

Is the relationship with your children on the basis of your being parents or a couple?

Your answer:

We all recognize that it would be terribly irresponsible for a couple to have a baby if they were not planning to have a relationship with one another. The child wouldn't have a fair start in life. There would be no stability. There would be no permanence, no security. But all too often we have children—and our intentions are fine—but in their growing years we don't provide them with any real relationship of us. We try to respond very meaningfully to them, but we put ourselves as a couple aside. Or we fit "us" into the time that's left over after we've taken care of our children.

Unfortunately, we make marriage a preliminary stage to parenthood. When the children come, we concentrate on being parents rather than on being married. We tend to take our marriage for granted and figure that it's going to be all right as long as we give it a minimum amount of attention. And we lose the greatest dimension of parenthood. We need to continue to concentrate on our marriage! When a husband and wife love one another, the children in that home grow with laughter on their lips and a song in their hearts. The old saying, "All the world loves a lover," is especially true of your children. They all love it when you're loving one another.

We go to all sorts of clinics for child psychology, we read

whatever we can to discover how we can be better parents and what our children's specific needs are. All those things have a certain value and nobody is putting them down. However, they're only meaningful in the context of our love for one another.

It is interesting to note the kind of answers that are given when you ask parents what they could do in order to become better parents. Many of their answers focus around some kind of self-improvement project such as being more patient or not yelling or making sure not to run out of peanut butter. Other answers deal with problem-solving. Something is going wrong in their understanding of their child or in their child's understanding of them, so there's straightening out to do.

We can believe intellectually that we're more concerned about our marriage than our parenthood and that our husband or wife is more important to us than our children, but our actions speak otherwise. We can even say that if it ever came to a choice, reluctantly but very definitely we would choose our wife or husband before our children—that we rank our marriage ahead of our parenthood. (It isn't simple to distinguish priorities in a real parent/child relationship. The children are a very real aspect of the marriage and essential to the expression of love between husband and wife—we won't be choosing our wife or our husband against our children if we have a true understanding of what the children are.)

However, no matter what we may say and no matter what we may honestly believe, we spend more of our attention and energy in trying to be good fathers and good mothers than we do on being good husbands and good wives. We let the children absorb us.

Let's examine ourselves. What are our ambitions and our hopes for the future? Isn't it true that we zero in on what our children are going to be like, who they're going to marry, what their life work is going to be, and whether or not they are going to live near us? We ask ourselves, "Will they take care of us when we are old, or will they cut us off?" Our dreams, our hopes and our ambitions indicate what's important to us.

111

They love it when we're loving one another.

A husband can say that his wife comes first and that's the reason why he's working so hard! A wife can feel that her husband comes before her children when she says, "My kids drive me up the wall. I'm so relieved to see my husband come home to have somebody to talk to!" But what does she talk about? She talks to him about the kids. Even when they do talk about other things, they discuss what has happened in the neighborhood and at the office or even in the world, which is fine, but it's about things; it's not about one another.

Personal communication between husband and wife doesn't happen often enough, deep enough, and overtly enough. There is a strong tendency in us to believe that our relationship is pretty well set. There are dissatisfactions, but we've pretty well learned to cope with them. We feel the thing to watch is our children because, after all, they're growing up. They're immature and inexperienced and there are many dangers in this world today. We are constantly talking over how we can do better by them now and provide better for them in the future. Not just materially, but personally.

Over the years our awareness of one another erodes, and our children gradually replace our love. When a husband asks for more attention from his wife, we may feel he's jealous of his own children. But maybe it isn't jealousy at all. Maybe it's an honest evaluation of something that's wrong in the home. When a wife wants to spend time with her husband rather than with their children, we may feel she's selfish and should be taking care of her responsibilities. But that's just it! Her prime responsibility is to her husband. His prime responsibility is to her. Putting each other first is the best way of fulfilling their responsibility to their children, and it's not selfish at all.

How wonderful for children to sense the coupleness of their parents! When we're facing into one another, they're dealing with one focus—a union of persons—a couple. When we live out our relationship on the basis of being single individuals, the children have two focuses. A mother and a father. That makes for difficulties.

Two girls came in to see me at different times on the same

day about their marriages. Their faces had the radiance that cosmetic companies promise but can't deliver.

Kathy was quite nervous. She wondered whether or not she would make a good wife. Was it too soon for her to settle down? Could she handle the many responsibilities later? She had a million questions, doubts and difficulties, and needed constant reassurance.

In Kathy's home, the kids came first. Her mom and dad were willing to put everything aside for the sake of the children. Kathy doesn't see the coupleness of her parents. She sees their services, their kindness, their efforts. She doesn't experience the core of it all—the two of them as a couple.

She's experiencing "couple" love now, but she sees the future as different and doesn't know how she's going to make it without her fiancé in the center. She wants to keep it that way, but feels guilty and troubled and fearful of future pressures.

Marlene was calm in the midst of her excitement. She had many of the same questions Kathy had, but she had confidence, and a peacefulness underlying all her feelings. Her parents communicated to the children the dominance of their love for one another. Marlene sensed the security as well as the thrill of coupleness.

It's very difficult to change our way of thinking. We've been brainwashed! We've been trained to be child-oriented. Why don't we give coupleness a chance? Let's have a go at it for six months or to see what the effect on the children will be. Let's make our marriage the prime relationship in the home. If the husband uses this as an escape from the children, or the wife feels it's an excuse not to pay attention to the kids, that's wrong. That's a negative thing. We're talking about something positive—a very real affirmation of our love for one another—an act of faith and trust.

The two of us are the nucleus around which our children satellite. Our children are an embodiment of our love for one another. But they are not the center. Our marriage—our oneness—has priority. We are the center. The fondest memory that our children should live with all their lives long is not all the things that we've done for them, all the love we've poured out on them, but all the love we've poured out on each other as husband and wife.

I'm going to reveal one of my reasons for having Marriage Encounter couples write love letters to each other.

On Christmas, Mom's birthday, Mother's Day, my dad would get a lovely present for my mother, but he also did something else that was very special. He'd write a long love note to her. The word would pass around that Daddy was writing to Mommy. Everything quieted down while he was at it. Mom always enjoyed the present, but the note she loved! She never let us read them, but we knew they meant the world to her. My dad has been dead for 30 years now, but whenever I think of him, and I do often, those love letters pop into my mind.

No child is going to lose by his parents' loving each other; he'll be more fully loved than ever. We'll be very aware that that child is *hers,* that child is *his.* We'll have a double motive for loving that child: because of who he is—our child—and because of who his mother or father is—our spouse. When we love a child because we love that boy's or girl's father or mother then we find him/her irresistible.

We can see this in just very simple incidents. The child of neighbors or friends about whom we care deeply get more understanding from us than a child whose parents we don't know. Our relationship with the child's parents carries over to the child himself. If that's true outside the home, it's true in our own home.

What is your child's greatest inheritance?   *Your answer:*

Believe it or not your child's greatest inheritance is your love for one another. This is very hard for us to comprehend be-

116

Marriage is the prime relationship in our house.

cause we have been taught that we must equip the child to face life. And to us that means to give our boy a great education, prepare our girl to stand on her own feet. We're proud when we are able to say, "He's going to make his way in life," and, "She'll be able to take care of herself." Our influence is taking hold; our training is having its effect. We can relax a little bit; we don't have to worry much anymore. We feel well on our way toward success in raising our children!

Yes, and maybe we would like, if we were in a good enough position, to be able to endow our children with money to live any kind of life they wanted. We want to make sure they have an easier time than we had.

But we've made more money in our lifetime than our parents ever made. Do we have fewer worries than they did? Do we have it any easier? Have we satisfied their plans for us to have a fun-filled life? And what about that education that they scrimped and saved and sweated to earn for us so that our life would be easier than theirs? We've used it instead to raise our goals and ambitions. We need more money for that "decent" standard of living, so we work as hard—or harder!

Maybe we ought to learn that more of the same is not the answer. And maybe we ought to come to grips with the reality that we have to have a whole different focus in life.

Suppose, just suppose, that our children were not as well equipped or maybe they were as well equipped but just not as urgent about making money as we have been. What if instead of being endowed with money-making potential, they were endowed with experiences and memories of our overwhelming love affair with one another? Isn't it just possible that their lives might be joy-filled? Isn't it in the realm of consideration that they might be able to actually find a full life and really enjoy it?

Everyone benefits from Dorothy and Larry's love. Dorothy is an old, old lady who is a dear friend of mine. When she was a girl she lived on Fifth Avenue in a big mansion. The house even had an elevator. (Imagine, having your very own elevator to play with!) Dorothy grew up, met and married Larry. He was a fine fellow but not what you would call a "success." Dorothy and Larry had to watch every penny. Those who "knew her when" are terribly sorry for Dorothy, but she is much happier than most of the people who are sorry for her! Larry passed away years ago, but she is still in love with him. She is full of his love. In her material poverty, she is a very wealthy lady. Every time she speaks his name, and she does frequently, she looks young again. You have to celebrate with her, her continuing joy in life and how much she has been loved.

Our basic problem is that we don't really believe in our love. In fact we have rather cynical sayings about love: love doesn't put food on the table; love is fine, but it doesn't pay the bills.

We tend to feel that love is for kids, and then we have to settle down and take over our responsibilities. But a mature, complete married love between a man and a woman is an ongoing beautiful romance and the best and the most life-giving experience that any child can ever have.

We're the richest country in the world. Yet the besetting atmosphere today is one of alienation. It's not going to be changed by our paying more attention to our children. We're going to bite into this deep malady only when we start really loving our spouse and loving our children because they come from our love for each other.

Do your children see you as individuals or as a couple?   *Your answer:*

How our children see us is not concerned with whether they have a good relationship with us, or whether we're satisfied with the way they're growing up. It is concerned with whether they are looking at us as a mother and a father who also just happen to be married, or as a couple—and that part of our coupleness is them. We don't have to be in perfect agreement on every decision in order for them to consider us a couple. We can sometimes disagree in front of the children. But, do they see "parents," or do they see "marriage"? Do they only see us in relationship with them, or do they see us in relationship with each other—as lovers?

A good way to find out is to ask our children to act out how they see us. These plays—or replays—can be quite illuminating.

If they automatically go into a busy-in-the-kitchen mother or a nose-in-the-newspaper father routine, then it should be pretty indicative to us that that's the dominant note we strike in the home. It may be that we come across as bread winner, professional, social activist, or neighborhood do-gooder for that matter. Then we're simply some vague characterization of an adult.

Or maybe we've fallen into the role of hassled bill payer, harried housewife or busy man- or woman-of-the-world instead of lovers. If our marriage is dominant in their minds, they'll act out Dad hugging Mom and Mom squeezing Dad and loving looks and lots of endearing terms.

A second test that we can take through our children is to ask them to act out how they see themselves! This will reveal the relationship they feel they have with us. They'll show us whether they deal with us separately or together, or if they have any real relationship with us at all. Maybe they'll reveal that their relationships outside the home are dominant, or that they have a solitary type of existence. Whatever way it comes out, we'll know more about how they see us.

How much do your children know about you as a couple?

Your answer:

One of the most frequent mistakes that good husbands and wives make is that they keep their married lives private from their children. Marriage becomes only something that takes place late at night, behind closed doors, or in the privacy of an intimate conversation. The public face the parents put on in front of their children is one in which their relationship is hidden.

Wouldn't it be good to let our children know the words we like to hear from one another, the things that cause secret little smiles in us, and what especially warms our heart when we look at our husband or our wife? Couldn't they know the pet names that we have for one another? Not just the common ones, but the really special ones that we have for each other?

Tom is 45 years old and bald, but one of the things that first attracted Nan to him was his curly, curly hair. When she's feeling particularly tender toward him, she smiles, reaches for his hand and calls him "Curly." One day 10-year-old Tommy said to his mother, "You know the nicest time to live in this house? It's when you call Daddy 'Curly.'"

Our children could know what we were thinking about in relationship to one another when we were planning to have each of them. They could know what pregnancy meant to us and what we talked about during the pregnancy—the way we communicated with one another while awaiting their birth.

Children love knowing everything about themselves. Their memories go back just so far, so any light we can cast on what happened to them before then means a great deal to them.

Betty realized how left out her son, Danny, felt when she came home with the second baby. She began to make a point of telling Danny what he had been like when he was inside of her. One day when he was tickled with his new sister's hiccoughs, Betty told him how he had hiccoughed a lot when he was in her tummy, and how she and Daddy had laughed and laughed to see her tummy wiggling like that. Danny grinned from ear to ear. He was tremendously pleased.

Couldn't we tell them what we experienced in one another when each of them was born? Are they aware that the wanting to have each of them came out of our choosing each other and a responsiveness to one another more than a conscious attraction to the child? Do they know what having them means to our relationship? The trust, the vulnerability involved?

How much do they really know us? Not just the externals, not just the specific characteristics of us and our spouse, but us as a couple? What do they feel holds us together? Do they know what we find precious about one another? What makes a difference to our love? Why we are continually choosing one another? Why this is the only man in the world for me? Why I could never be satisfied with any other woman? What it is like to think about being without one another? What it is like to sleep alone? What we talk about when we're by ourselves at night? Why I am different since I met and married this wonderful person?

Maybe the children should know how tenderly we love one another. Then we could show our affection for one another in front of the children. Maybe our children should know that we make love. Actually, the best form of sex education is for a good and loving husband and wife to talk openly with their children about what it means to a husband and wife to have one another.

Our sexual love is a gift we can share beautifully with our children by just talking about our own love, our own hopes and fears, our own joys and disappointments. When we teach sex as the facts of life or just give our children a set of "do's and don'ts" they get all mixed up. We don't need to discuss with them the mechanics of sex, the positions or other physical details. We do need to share what communicating with each other as a husband and wife means to us and our spouse. How we have doubts and fears and work very hard to understand one another. We can share that we don't always understand ourselves, and how we help each other.

The whole philosophy behind this book is a heartfelt belief that the best thing for kids is their parents, most specifically, in their love for one another. If your children are formed in their sexual attitudes by becoming aware of what you mean to one another, how can they ever be casual about sex? We are not satisfied with the sex education we now have, so this way offers hope.

**What do you want
your children
to learn from you?**

Your answer:

It would be interesting to write out the things that strike our minds when we start thinking about what we want to teach the children. There's a whole kaleidoscope of things—how to be good citizens; how to be responsible people, independent; how to be able to earn a living; how to have a happy, satisfying life.

When you come right down to it why would a child have to grow up with parents who are married? All these things could be provided by a single parent or by people who have professionally taken on the responsibility of providing the physical and mental well-being of today's youth. Maybe in the past there were economic and sociological reasons why marriage was a necessity for having children, but they aren't valid anymore. All those things can be provided in other ways.

So again we come back to the question, "Why should there be any necessity for a *couple* in the upbringing of a child?" Certainly a couple has no corner on the market of goodness. Single men and women are very good and sincere people. So why should it be a couple? Is it just a legal nicety? Is it just for propriety's sake? Is it just because that's the way it has always been done, and we couldn't think of doing otherwise? Or maybe we think that marriage is old-fashioned, but we feel stuck with the traditions of the past, and we're not radical enough to buck against the way we've always been taught.

There's only one reason that holds water. There's only one contribution that a couple can make to the life of their child that cannot be made by anyone else. That is their love for one another. If a couple doesn't offer that to their children then they're failing in their prime responsibility, for the one thing that distinguishes them from other people is their relationship with each other.

Whatever each of them may bring to the home, whatever skills or talents or capabilities, they're all nothing compared with the one overriding calling they have in their lives to love each other. The one thing that their children need more than anything else for their proper nurturing and upbringing is a husband and wife who really love each other.

Parenthood has to be an expression of coupleness, not a replacement for it, not an addition to it, not a sideline, not an end in itself. Our children speak by their very existence who we are to one another.

PARENTS ARE TO GIVE LIFE— CONTINUALLY.

4

LIFE-GIVING

What makes you a parent?

Your answer:

A parent is one who has given, and is giving, life. All the other things that are involved, the responsibilities and duties in taking care of the needs of the child, have to fit into that one overriding reality. Parents give life to their child. Furthermore, giving life is not something that is over and done with. As parents, we are called to be life-giving in all of our dealings with our children.

Unfortunately we tend to lose sight of this fact. Every human being is tremendously impressed and awed by the power to give life. The moment of birth is an extremely tremendous experience. But as the child grows we lose sight of the life-giving aspects of our relationship. We look at the chores, and they become a drudgery. We begin to take that life for granted.

The way we look at ourselves and how we usually think of parenting indicates how far life-giving is from our minds. Unless we've just had a baby, we don't think very much at all about "giving life." We think about education, homework, and shoes, clothes, and all sorts of everyday things. They are necessary, but only meaningful when they fit into the core of what parenthood is all about—the giving of life.

We don't realize that we are just as much called to give life to our children today as we did 5, 10, or 45 years ago. We think that our job is to conserve the life of our child. We do not see that we are continually being given the opportunity to initiate life in the child. Here is an opportunity for a very special relationship with each of our children.

What effect does a duty-oriented mentality have on parents?

Your answer:

Parents who are duty-oriented can be very cautious and quite nervous. They recognize that their children are a tremendous responsibility, and because they are sincere and really worthwhile people, they want desperately to live up to that responsibility.

They become aware of all the mistakes they make, of all the dangers that can beset their children. And parents tend to be very harsh on themselves. They blame themselves constantly. They set a level of performance for themselves that they're constantly scrambling to live up to and act out.

They're constantly estimating how well their children are growing and maturing and living up to what is expected of them. Implicitly behind that evaluation of the child's performance is a very real analysis of their own performance as parents.

Because we love our children dearly, and because we want them to have the fullest possible life for themselves now and in the future, we set very high standards for them and for us —standards that are impossibly high. However, parenthood should be focused on persons and those persons in relationship, not on performance.

Lori is well-mannered, helpful, reliable, and very nervous. She picks up every mistake she makes and magnifies it. She has picked that up from her folks. They are very conscientious people, constantly striving to do the right thing. Their focus is on how Lori is acting. She never gets a chance to be a person, to let her hair down, to be herself. She is always on duty.

After one semester Lori's report card had a couple marks below her usual A's. Her dad was disappointed and started to lecture her on studying more when his eyes caught hers and saw the sadness in her. He said instead, "Lori, I've been spoiled. I've grown so used to your high marks that I've taken them for granted. I needed this report card to really appreciate how lucky I am to have you." Her eyes brimmed with tears as she said, "Thank you, Dad, I'd hoped you'd understand me."

If a couple looks at marriage and doesn't concentrate on the "you" in their relationship, it's not going to be a love relationship. Rather, it's going to be a dutifully carrying out of activities and obligations. The result is that the husband or wife, or both of them, will see themselves as tremendous failures in the marriage.

It can also happen in the parent-child relationship when we're not looking at the child, but at the performance chart. We're so busy measuring the child against our unreasonable standards that we inevitably see ourselves as failures.

A friend of mine used to act that way with his son, Paul. If Paul seemed to watch television too much, or the neighbors got upset with him over some boyish boisterousness, or was in a bad mood one day, Del took it to heart. He was too good a man to blame the boy all the time. He blamed himself. He was not a good enough father. He didn't spend enough time with the boy. He wasn't sensitive enough.

The real problem was neither Del nor his son. It was those standards that he thought he constantly had to have the boy live up to. He looked on being a father as a job instead of a call to just love Paul.

Is there an element of selfishness in being duty-oriented?   *Your answer:*

Looking at life as "doing my duty" is a self-perfection project. We look at ourselves to see how we rate as a father, as a mother. It's understandable and it's part of our goodness, but we're exaggerating our self-importance. We feel we have a responsibility to be a certain way, that it's part of our integrity, that we must live up to our obligations. We take our eyes off our children and put them on ourselves.

This can be subtle. Our minds can be quite filled with thoughts of our children. We can honestly believe that the motivation for all our choices, decisions and actions is their well-being. But at the root of our behavior is our wanting what's best for them because we're supposed to want what's best for them. We feel it is part of the task that we have as parents. Sometimes when we seem to be very other-centered, we're actually very self-centered.

We sometimes make our children the basis of the way we view ourselves. If they're not doing well, then we consider ourselves to be failures. If everything is going smoothly, then

132

we look on ourselves as successful. We are "involved" with the children, but still not necessarily having any *relationship* with them. That isn't parenting.

What main element goes into life-giving parenthood?

Your answer:

A man and woman are husband and wife before they are mother and father. Their parenthood is an expression of their coupleness. Tragically, we separate the two. We wear different hats. One as a couple; the other as parents. We shouldn't.

The success that we achieve as parents is determined by the success we have in our relationship with one another. If we're convinced of our oneness, and living it out, our relationship with our children will be in the same area of our life with our relationship with our wife or husband.

However, if our children are simply a result of our coming together one moment in time, and our dealings with them are completely apart from our relationship with one another, then the environment is over-child-oriented. A conflict is created between the marital and the parental relationships. This is detrimental to our children.

It's like a person who has only one eye. What he sees, he sees very clearly and he doesn't even realize what he's not seeing. So, too, with a child who is dealing with his mother, his father—individually—on a one-to-one basis. What he's experiencing may be good and satisfying in itself, but there's a whole side of things that is not visible to him.

What he's missing is the perspective of his parents as a couple. When it's mother and child—or father and child—the relationship has to be established. When it's husband and wife

133

—together—and child, the relationship has already been created, the child is part of it and has been all his life—he shares in an ongoing love!

When we recognize how vital the marriage relationship is, the parent one becomes viable and successful.

What does a child bring to a couple for their own relationship?

Your answer:

A child certainly helps a couple see that their relationship is not a static one. Conception, birth, and especially the continuing to give life makes the relationship dynamic and creative. Husband and wife are not just biological parents; their love is that child. They can pick it up, they can touch it, they can hug and kiss their love.

The physical and biological event of parenthood is a symptom of another miracle—the two of them giving of themselves to one another. The creation of the child is the result and outpouring of the two creating a fuller life with and for one another.

Actually, thinking about children is only a dreamy type of thing, at first. It isn't until a couple meets and falls in love that they start thinking meaningfully about having children. Then their thinking is not children in the abstract, or just any child. It's having *his* child, *her* child, that makes having children exciting and beautiful. Their love for one another is the attraction that causes them to want children. Their love is so special and magnificent that it cannot be contained! It must express itself in a life, and thus their love becomes immortal.

134

**How do life-giving
parents look at
each other?**

Life-giving parents are concerned with giving their children's life in the *present* moment. This is more than just keeping them in life. The life they give to their children is the outpouring of their relationship with one another—their coupleness. More than anything else, the child needs to experience the together love of the husband and wife.

The whole creative process was begun by the love of that couple, and the creative process will continue as long as that love continues and develops. The real fullness of life at any given moment is dependent upon the relationship between this man and this woman who have committed themselves by the creation of their child to continue to give life to him.

Many of us fall into the trap of trying to simplify complex things, of wanting to shrink long-term dimensions to once-and-for-all moments. We look on marriage as an event that's past—and now we have to live out the consequences. We feel the same way as far as our children are concerned. They are a result of an action we performed, and now we have to live out the consequences. If we think this, then we've missed the whole point.

Marriage shouldn't be that way at all. Marriage isn't ever accomplished, it's always being accomplished. We're always marrying one another.

Couples after a Marriage Encounter weekend are excited. They have discovered that their wedding day was only the first day of their marriage—that every day they marry each other a little bit more. Marriage is not something done. It is a process. It's always being done. It's an evolving thing. Their marriage is how much they are aware of one another and absorbed in one another each day.

135

"Every day I'm marrying you a little bit more."

We can't live off a wedding pledge that we made 20 or 40 years ago. We have to be constantly renewing it. At the time we made that pledge we had no full awareness of what it meant. We only knew the persons of us that were 20 years ago. We're much more than that now. Therefore we're capable of a much deeper pledge. Because of the love that we have exercised toward one another over the years, our love potential is much greater. To limit marriage to the horizons we had when we first pledged ourselves to one another is sad. There's a beautiful old saying: "I love you more than yesterday and less than tomorrow." Whoever wrote that had a genuine awareness of the growth of love.

The same thing is true as far as our children are concerned.

We're never parents; we're always becoming parents. It's an evolving thing. It's a process, not a static fact. We have more life to give our children than when they were first created. We gave everything we had, and that was enough for the moment. But it's not enough now. We have so much more of our love to share with them. To expose them to, to reveal to them, to allow them to participate in, to envelop them with.

We know that if we had not come together physically, there would be no child. But unless we are coming together spiritually now, with our children and in heart, then the child will be deprived of some of the life that he has a right to expect.

Life-giving is something that goes way beyond physical life. It's not based on doing more and more for our children, it's based on giving more and more of ourselves to one another! Each day, we become more open to one another and more loving with one another. The life that we give to our children is never our own individually. It's the life and love of us as a couple.

Mimi and Jack have a lovely practice at Sunday dinner. They tell their three little ones what they have learned about their marriage the past week. One Sunday Mimi shared what she had learned about Jack's even temper. She confessed that in the past she hadn't been terribly pleased with that quality of his. In fact, sometimes it had made her want to scream. She had wished he'd show some reaction—even if he had to yell. She had thought he was cold and unfeeling. The past week she had seen for the first time what a gift he was to her that way. All the children had been down with mumps; there had been a flood in the basement; Grandma was staying with them; and a check had bounced! Jack didn't get ruffled. He was there, steady and sure, for her to lean on. Somehow she had begun to realize that he, too, was upset, that he had deliberately kept himself calm for her sake. She realized now how much freedom he gave her to let go, to react, to be herself, by his tranquility. She had always thought before that he didn't care. Now she saw that it was precisely because he did care that he was that way. It wasn't the things that were happening that determined his reaction. It was she. Mimi explained that her new understanding made her love Daddy more and more. The kids were wide-eyed. They were in on their parents' love.

Life-giving parents are focused in on their relationship with one another, and it's that relationship with one another that is in relationship with their children, giving them life.

The more in love we are with one another, the greater closeness we experience with one another, the better off the kids are. We are their neighborhood. We are their environment. Everyone wants the children to have a good atmosphere in which to grow up. That's us!

How do life-giving parents look at their children?   *Your answer:*

There are external and internal aspects of continuous life-giving. Most obvious are the physical and biological aspects, but life-givingness must be more than putting food into the children's mouths. And the atmosphere that's provided by the service we give our children must come from something other than our playing the role of a mother, a father.

It is this husband and this wife caring for their children's needs as an expression of their care for each other. They care with the strength of the other's love. It's not feeding a child, it's feeding *his* child. It's not bandaging a little girl's knee, it's bandaging *her* girl's knee. Above all, it's not doing good things for *my* children, it's for *our* children—or better yet—*his* children, *her* children. The children are flesh of his flesh, bone of his bone.

Did you ever notice when you talk about the children how often you refer to them as *my* children? We can say to ourselves that it's just a slip of the tongue, but when we try to change that slip of the tongue, we find out how much our relationship with our children is strictly as singles!

We recognize that our spouse has a part in parenting, but each of us has his own relationship with the children. We may be tempted to say, "Well, what's so wrong about that? How can we possibly relate to them in any other way?" There has to be another way, because there's an element missing. It is the love relationship between husband and wife. That should be the prime element in the home. Then the couple can focus on the children.

We're not talking about externals—the direct dealing with the child—the action, the words, the non-verbal communication that passes between a parent and child. We are considering a point of view, how we look at parenthood. Whose child is this? We can say that we know the children are ours. We were together. He had a part in having them, of course. She bore them and gave birth to them and now does so much for them. Yes, but whose children are these at any precise moment when I'm relating to them? We're talking about a frame of mind. We don't have to say all the time, "Well, now, whenever I'm talking to you, your father is talking to you, too," or, "If I'm playing ball with you, it's really your mother and I playing catch with you."

We need to realize that just as life cannot be created and transmitted singly initially, neither can it be given singly on a continuing basis after the child has been born. It takes two to give life. We must love our children in terms of our spouse, specifically because this child is *his,* this child is *hers.* Even on the straight physical and biological plane, life has to be an expression of the relationship between husband and wife rather than being just a direct service to the child. If it is only a direct meeting of the child's needs, then it's life maintenance. It's not life-giving.

Is life-giving only important for the child?   *Your answer:*

Gramps still talks about Grandma.

Parents who are life-givers benefit as much or more than their children. The quality of giving life is so core, so essential to a man and a woman that unless they are giving life, they are sterile and unfulfilled. There is an old saying that love isn't love until you give it away. There's a deep meaning behind that. Love stagnates unless it's constantly moving outward. Love is not something that can be stored up. And an essential part of love is giving life.

It's not true that the only way love is life-giving is by the physical creation of a child. We look on ourselves as life-giving—and expect it of ourselves—in the conception and birth of a child. We must look on ourselves to continually give life from the beginning of our children into their full manhood and womanhood—till the end of our lives.

There's a need in people, especially in the elderly, to experience life—to feel life coursing under their fingertips. This is such a human urgency that when our children are on their own we fill the vacuum in our lives with our grandchildren— or pets—or plants. We need to care for someone or something.

In the overall picture we consider ourselves life preservers rather than life creators. We have as much life in our love for one another to give to our children when they're 16 as when they were first conceived. When we believe that parenting children is a "taking care of" type of thing, then we look on ourselves as out of a job when they reach 21 or get their first employment. Actually, each stage of the development of our children merely changes the way we express our love for one another to them. Whether they've grown out of the diaper stage or can feed themselves or cross the street on their own or ride a bus to school or have families of their own, we can indicate to them through our parenthood that they are a gift to us from our beloved husband or wife.

I was discussing this point with a group of couples when one husband gave a perfect example. He began raving about his father. "That old man is the world's greatest lover. All my life long he hasn't been able to be with me two minutes without talking about my mother. When I was a kid he got me a set of trains. Every time we set them up, he would tell me about the train trips he took with Mom. He had all sorts of funny stories about her hat boxes. When I was older, I had a tough time with my dates, because when I took them home to meet my folks, all they could talk about was how much my mom and dad loved one another. Now my kids are impressed. They want me to talk about Terry the way Gramps talks about Grandma. And there's more to it. Whenever he's around, I feel full and complete. I discover all sorts of hopes and dreams hidden inside me that I never knew I had. I really become a new man every time I see him."

People treasure keepsakes because they are precious to them. They hang on to a faded old photograph, a bedraggled book with a signature inside the front cover, or a love note. But children are the greatest keepsakes that we have. We can say to our spouse, "For the sake of keeping me in mind I give you our children."

Now isn't it tragic when someone forgets the giver and gets totally absorbed in the gift? The gift in itself is nice and wonderful but the real meaning is because of the giver. The same thing is true with our children. The real meaning in those children is because they come from our husband, our wife.

So children should not be things that bind us together in a mutual responsibility, but a memento of one another. Every time we deal with our children, we can be reminded of our love for one another.

Charlie is a teenager I know who is the spitting image of his father in more ways than one. Physically, yes. And some of his head mannerisms and his smile are carbon copies of Dave's. But the even greater similarities are his qualities. He has the same bemused, easy-going, half-serious—but wholly sincere—view of life. He is completely reliable, eager to please, highly talented.

His mother says that she can't talk with Charlie without seeing Dave in him. She is continually reminded of how much Dave means to her and how much she loves him.

She and Charlie have a great relationship because he's not on his own with her. She has loved him in Dave long before he was ever born. No matter what he says or does she understands him because of what she knows about Dave. Charlie really has it made and always will.

Unfortunately, over the years we lose sight of our marital relationship and replace it with our parental one. We even think of each other as "mother" or "father," rather than "my beloved." We allow the children—who should be the expression and the reminder of our love—to become the focus of our love. Instead of the children getting their identity from our relationship with one another, we get our identity from our relationship with them! That's backwards. Instead of our children causing us to be more conscious of one another,

142

more responsive to one another, more tightly knit with one another, they pull us apart, become a distraction, sometimes even a replacement.

On the other hand if we recognize that their lives have only begun and we have much more of our life to give them, then we will never misdirect our prime husband/wife relationship. The greatest need our children have is strictly us. Yes, very definitely they need us to be responsive to them personally and individually, but only in terms of our prior, basic relationship with one another. That's the life that has to be given to them; the life of "us" that we are presently creating.

What aspects of life-giving, other than the physical, are important?   *Your answer:*

We've become aware, especially in this generation, that all the physical care in the world is not enough for good health. Nor are all the services we give our children. One of the reasons why so many people have the self-centered notion that people are there to take care of them and to do things for them is because that's the fundamental relationship they have experienced in their homes. They don't ever really look for a mature person-to-person relationship with others.

Emotional and psychological dimensions call for fulfillment. A person's needs in these areas are fundamentally responded to by experiences of being understood. Basically, the giving of life to our children on these terms is going to be accomplished by listening to them.

Our children's lives also have an intellectual dimension for which we have to make a provision. The education that our schools provide is a technical education; the curriculum is designed to teach the tools of the trade. The schools are not teaching how to be human. They can't. Only a good home can. So we are the prime educators! We have to be concerned with the basic education that every human being needs—and that is to be a lover. We can give them exposure to people who love one another. Then gradually the experience of the love they breathe will become part of the fabric of their beings.

Then there's the spiritual aspect of life-giving. If the children are experiencing the constant total love between their mother and father, it's going to be very simple for them to be whole persons.

If our children get a real sense that they are our ambassadors to the world to speak out the beauty of who we are to one another, they will never have any problem with their purpose in life. And we will be giving life rather than merely giving existence.

We can tell our children over and over that they're special and that they're different from everybody else on the face of this earth, but they're going to find it very difficult to believe. They're going to say, "Why? How am I different?" We can tell them they are different by being our love incarnate. Our children are our words to communicate our love to the world.

What are the essential elements in life-giving?

Your answer:

Life-givingness can begin with as simple a thing as listening. Listening is terribly important in any human relationship. We have to listen to our children verbally and non-verbally. But if we're doing a poor job of listening to one another then we're going to listen poorly to our children, too. If we're just listening to one another in terms of hearing the words of finding out what we're supposed to be doing for each other, then that's the way we're probably listening to our kids. If we are really listening to our spouse and our children, then we have faced into one of the most essential elements of life-giving.

Forgiving and seeking forgiveness is another essential element in giving life to our children. Forgiving our children can sometimes be a problem. When they hurt us, we may let it go, and tell them it's OK. But then we store it up. We don't forget, and when the child does something similar again we bring it up—again and again. It can seem to the child that he is carrying a life sentence.

Forgiveness is always a two-way street. One party has to seek forgiveness and the other has to grant it. Just getting the child to admit he's wrong has not accomplished forgiveness.

Forgiveness focuses on the healing that takes place in the person who has offended. Too often we concentrate on the healing of the offended party, and that is not forgiveness at all. When a person says, "I'm sorry," that's a step forward, but that's not forgiveness either. Forgiveness is the recognition of the goodness of the person who is seeking forgiveness. Our child has given us a great gift by seeking our forgiveness; we can forget the fault and prize the moment of reconciliation. What we should be most aware of is not the hurt we experienced but the healing that takes place in the offender. So, in granting forgiveness to our children, we don't want to say it's over with. Instead, "We'll never forget this moment." We don't want to brush aside what has happened and start off as if nothing has happened. Something magnificent has happened! Forgiveness has been sought; we can never be the same again! And it seems especially hard for us to come out and say, especially to a child, "Forgive me." We don't want to admit being wrong, and we're concerned with keeping the child's respect. Actually, we earn the greatest possible respect by admitting that we can fail. We give our child dignity and worth in his own eyes when he sees it reflected from ours— when he knows we consider him to be a person of dignity and worth, and this is true equality when we can say to our children that we've been wrong.

Praising and complimenting our children are important. Too often we pass over the good things our children do and just expect that that's the way things should be. We may give an offhanded expression of praise or gratitude but not zero in and really compliment that particular boy or girl for being so good. Maybe one of the reasons we find it difficult to take compliments is because we hear them so seldom. We don't know how to handle them. We really don't want our children to be the same way we are as far as receiving compliments is concerned, so let's give them some practice!

Being open and sharing about ourselves is a very important element in life-giving. One of the questions that we must face is, "How familiar are our children with our relationship? Do they know about how much we mean to one another, how much we're entwined with one another?" We really have to recognize that it's our marriage that gives life to our children. Consequently they have to be involved in our marriage, they have to be aware of our love for one another. We can say to ourselves, "Well, of course they see that. They see that we're affectionate with one another, that we really care for one another, that we listen to one another." Yes, that's true and that's a good start. But all too often there are dimensions of our lives that we don't share. We may talk together one way when we're by ourselves and another way when we're with the children. I once went to the wake of a close friend. Afterwards her grown children brought me back to their house for a cup of coffee. The three of them were very sad, not just because of the loss by death. The oldest boy said, "You know I've learned more about Mom and Dad in the last two days since she died than in all my 31 years." His sister added, "I never really knew before how much Mom and Dad talked and what was really important to them. They didn't talk about themselves." With tears in his eyes, their younger brother said, "I feel cheated. Dad shouldn't have kept Mom to himself. They had so much, but all they talked about in front of us was us. It's as though we didn't belong in any way to the most important part of their lives."

To be life-giving, we have to be open and sharing of ourselves.

In what ways can you be "anti-life"?

Not listening, not being forgiving or asking forgiveness, not praising or being open with our children, is being anti-life by default. The first and most significant out-and-out enemy of life-givingness is criticism. There's nothing that stunts life more, nothing that destroys life more, than criticism. How frequently and how devastatingly we criticize our children! We do it in such an offhanded way, without thinking too much about it!

Why do we do it? How can we criticize his gift, her offering to us? Criticism says that we've lost sight of the fact that this child is his, is hers. We could never criticize that which is our beloved's if we were considering our love for one another.

So, once again the problem is in our relationship with one another, or in our not recognizing that our children are an expression of our oneness. It's not as simple as just saying, "Well, I won't criticize anymore." We have to get to the root of our criticism. What are we saying about our relationship with our husband and wife when we criticize the children?

Another anti-life experience we thrust upon a child is to compare him with somebody else. This comparison may be subtle or overt, it may be implicit or it may be very explicit. The comparison might be with us when we were his age or with a brother or sister. There's no way that he can compete under those circumstances. There's no way that she can appreciate herself.

When we make comparisons, we are saying to our child that he will only please us if he becomes someone else, that who he is is not who we want him to be. Or we're telling him that his brother or sister, this other expression of our love for one another, is a better symptom of our relationship with each other than he is. It really is devastating when we look at it that way, isn't it? We're rejecting the child, taking away his identity, asking him to give up who he is, making him less because he's not somebody else.

147

We listen and Ted knows we understand.

We don't usually make the comparisons in big ways, and we're certainly not conscious of taking away the child's identity. We do it in little things like, "Why can't you brush your teeth like your sister?" Or, "Why can't you keep your room as neat as your brother does?" Or, "The other kids in the family have always done their homework, why can't you?" This also has the negative effect of reducing and interfering with the child's relationship with the other members of the family. It is hard for a little girl who's just been put down in comparison with her sister or brother to be very loving and open with that sister or brother.

Probably the most subtle aspect of being anti-life is living the future for our children. We keep looking ahead to what they have to become, to what they have to be prepared to face, to what skills and abilities they need to have two years from now or ten years from now. This can be the worst comparing of all. We have an ideal in our minds of what that boy or that girl has to be as an adult, so we treat them now in terms of what we see they must become.

We all laugh about the silliness of the kindergarten teacher who sends home a report card with the comment that the child is immature. Of course the child is immature. He's supposed to be immature. He's only five years old!

All of us do the same thing. We have a planned outline in our minds of how the child should progress. We very carefully evaluate in our minds how this child is developing the self-reliance we want him to have. We pressure him to get high enough marks to get into the college we've chosen. We judge him continually. Is he kind enough, tough enough, articulate enough to be the type of person we want him to be?

We're looking at parenthood as a task that's been assigned to us (or that we have assumed) that has to come out a certain way. We're dealing with the flesh-and-blood child as he is now. We're looking past that child into the years to come. But wait a minute. We can't build a present relationship with our child on a future possibility or even a probability. We can only deal with the child as he is right now. If we're so involved with the future, trying to mold him into what he can't be now, whether he ever becomes that or not, then we're bypassing the beauty and the wonder and uniqueness that is our boy or girl at this present moment.

Not only are we depriving the child, but we're really depriving ourselves. We're missing a wonderful opportunity to enjoy our children. We say to ourselves, "When the job is done we can really enjoy them." But how are we going to do that when we haven't had any practice? We're going to continue doing what we've been doing for the first 21 years. We'll keep on trying to make them into the kind of persons we believe our sons and daughters should be.

Again, as always, it comes back to our relationship; so often we're trying to improve our children beyond the point we ourselves have reached. We want them to be different than we were or are.

In these circumstances we're treating our children as separate entities rather than as an integrated part of our love.

We may sometimes fool ourselves into believing that we're not acting that way—because we don't see ourselves setting high goals for our children. But we could be less obvious. We might not be demanding about marks, but we might be insistent and demanding when it comes to fun or relaxation. We can be treating them as adults in not giving them guidelines or ground rules to help provide limits within which they can make decisions on their own level.

Actually, it is tremendously freeing for the parents to focus in on the children as they are and not be constantly having to nudge them the next step. It gives us a chance to just delight in them. That is life-giving! Our children will be at their best more and more as we find joy in them.

Are your decisions for your children based on what is right—or what is life-giving?

Your answer:

All of us want to do the right thing for our children. So we ask, "Is this or that right? Are we going to spoil them? Are we going to give them too much, or too little? Are we too strict? Are we too lenient?" So, many good people go through agonies in making decisions trying to discover how to be doing right by their kids.

Suppose parents just thought about life-giving, and they asked themselves whether the moment called for a punishment or a reward, a restriction or a gift. What would be the most life-giving thing at this time with Johnny or Mary?

The difficulty with trying to be right all the time is that we're facing out from the child, trying to evaluate the effect on the child. We're concerned with what we've been told by a child psychiatrist, or with what other people do, or with what's going to win the approval of somebody else. We might just be thinking about the child in relation to the future. We really aren't focusing in on the child at this moment.

On the other hand, our relationship to the child in the context of being life-giving changes our whole attitude. We ask ourselves, "How much of an allowance will be life-giving? Is our going to bed or waiting up for him at the end of his first date more life-giving? Is it life-giving to let our teenager drive the family car?" The list could go on and on. We can truly develop a life-giving mentality in the decisions that we make concerning our children.

The truth of the matter is that we can afford to risk a lot more when we're trying to give life to our children than when we're trying to be "right" about them. We can be much less rigid and strict. We're not implying that permissiveness is always life-giving. There are occasions when it might well be more life-giving to give a gentle no than a compliant yes.

How much do you allow parents and neighbors to influence your relationship with your children?   *Your answer:*

It is a natural temptation to lean on the experience of others, and there's nothing particularly wrong with doing so. However, it is not life-giving for our children to have us trying to please our mother or father or our neighbors, even if all of them are in agreement. We may know that we're going to get criticized if we don't do with our children what these people expect us to do. Consequently, we may include in our

151

decision-making process advice from other sources, too: current magazines, child psychology books, the children's teachers.

It isn't that we shouldn't read these books or magazines or that we shouldn't ask advice and direction of other people, but we really have to recognize that what comes first is the *relationship* with the child, not the correctness of the decision. We may get very accurate, helpful advice from other people, but if it doesn't fit into our couple/child relationship then it's not life-giving. How is our decision, how is our discipline, how is our punishment, how is our lifestyle in the home going to affect our children's awareness of us as a couple? How much is it going to make them more trusting of us, more willing to listen to us, more willing to be open with us? Those are the real questions that have to be faced and that's where we find great joy in being parents.

Are your punishments life-giving?   *Your answer:*

Our punishments are usually act-oriented and seldom life-giving. The punishment is act-oriented in the sense that it's focused in on something that the child is doing or not doing. So, fundamentally, when we're dealing with punishments, we're centering around getting an activity corrected.

There's no question that we can't just allow our children to go around hitting their playmates with baseball bats or running across the street without looking for cars. We do want the child to stop the activity, but we should want him to stop it not only because of the problems involved for the child, but because he sees that it's an improper expression of his relationship with us. If our relationship with our children is not

152

There's nothing like enjoying the children *now*.

on that level, or if their understanding of what our relationship is all about has not matured to that point, we may well have to interfere with their activities through some punishment or threat of punishment. That is necessary but inadequate; that is an emergency procedure at best. Ultimately we want to get our children to see that their lives are not just avoiding bad things and doing good things, but that their lives are for loving.

We want them not just to respect the rights of others, but to positively reach out to others and bring happiness to them, their brothers and sisters, their friends, their teachers, etc. We want them to see what a gift they are in themselves and how much they have within them to contribute personally to the joy of other people.

It's important to recognize that there is a big difference between discipline and punishment. We frequently equate the two. When we discipline the children we're trying to get them to do what we want them to do. When we punish them, we're making them pay for a family crime.

The best discipline we can give our children is to help them recognize the love we have for one another—the love which has created them. We want them to live up to that love, not in terms of compulsion, or coercion, but in terms of responsiveness and opportunity. The highest motivation for a child to do right is to think to himself, "I couldn't let my folks down," or, "This would please Mom and Dad."

What about teenagers?   *Your answer:*

Our teenagers have a very special place in our lives. Unfortunately it's not always a very positive one. The attitude that tends to be expressed toward teenagers, and one that they face from the time they're able to understand the word "teen" tends to be a rejecting one. The child grows up hearing his mother's friend say to her, "Wait 'til he becomes a teen, he's nice and sweet now, but . . . oh, boy!"

We develop self-fulfilling prophecies so that a boy or girl grows up thinking a teenager is a very special problem category. The moment he walks down the stairs on his 13th birthday he has become someone different from who he's always been in the family.

All those casual comments that we pass at the table about teenagers today, accumulate over the years in the child's mind and heart. A boy or girl might be very faithful and loyal and loving, but we keep looking for signs that they're just like the other teens or that they're going to be drawn into the trap by their schoolmates or what they read in the newspapers or see on television.

Actually, our teenagers are an even fuller expression of our love for one another than our little ones. They are starting to become aware of what a man and woman can mean to one another, so they are able to understand us better.

We're not trying to be naive here and say that there aren't

special problems connected with teens. Teenagers are beginning to become full-fledged adults. They are beginning to question things and to recognize that they have responsibility to be the kinds of persons they are called to be. This can sometimes cause friction between parents and children. However, if we're open to them, take time to listen to them, and are responsive, they are more capable of loving us and of being responsive to us than they have ever been in their lives.

Remember how delighted we were when there was noticeable advancement in our children, like the first step or the first word? That should be our reaction to our teenagers. This is positive. This is life-giving!

Do your children know how you make decisions concerning them?

Your answer:

Many children see only the results of decision-making. A situation comes up. We tell them what our decision is. It may well be that we foresaw the situation, analyzed it, prayed over it, wrestled with it, looked deeply inside ourselves, talked it over late into the night—but they don't know that we did.

So, on the one hand, children look on us as gods who have an incredible capability to divine decisions instantaneously. On the other hand, if a decision was slow in coming, they believe that we didn't think it was worth much effort and didn't take it seriously.

Of course we do take seriously and sincerely anything that affects our children. But they don't know that unless we allow them to experience what leads up to a decision. They may on a few occasions been aware that we had to work out a solution, but the effort may have come across to them as neces-

Fun at the table—especially
with Serendipity placemat games.

sary because there was a disagreement between us rather than as our having a sincere desire to approach with care anything that affects them. We can start making our decisions in front of them, working the situation out with one another in their presence. It's going to make a great deal of difference to our children if they know how seriously we treat everything about them. It's going to be a life-giving time for them to feel the intensity of our caring and to actually see and experience our decision-making.

It is beautiful to see the reaction of children when parents expose themselves this way. They say, "My mom and dad care for me. I'm that important." That's a great way to bring new life to that child.

What are some practical ways to bring more life to your children?   *Your answer:*

Our days are filled with action; everyone in a family might have a different schedule. But just possibly we can attract everyone to one spot at one time. Family mealtime has its own special drawing power. Maybe at breakfast we're all together. Maybe at dinner the family is at home. We can make the atmosphere at the table so happy, so vibrant and worthwhile that it will be a life-giving experience.

"But there's television, there's Little League, there's dancing class, there's homework to do—and not everyone is going to be home, anyway," we say. We could go on and on with the list of activities that hinder or interrupt our having meals together as a family.

Mealtime can be more than a slapdash meal put together on a counter with no thought or care for anyone but to grab a bite as he hurries by; mealtime can be a special event. Then it can come alive.

The family meal is, in a sense, the liturgy of the home. We can make it something meaningful, interesting and delightful. If we don't, if we give up the family meal, we could be giving up the heartland of our home.

Another real and vital aspect of giving life to our children is by giving them their history. Tell them something about the land their forefathers came from and the beautiful customs and beliefs and values the people in that land had and why they came to this country. We can incorporate the songs and practices from the old country into some of the family mealtimes. Such times can bring a couple and their children closer together and build memories.

All too often we pay attention to nutrition and to balanced diet, and we don't give any real life to our children at our meals. We forget that we are the best nutrition for one another.

What are the goals of a life-giving relationship between parents and child?   *Your answer:*

The first goal in life-giving is to enlarge the child's capacity to experience and enjoy his present life. The second is to instill in the child a sense of being part of us. The third, to create many memorial moments of closeness between us and the child. Fourth, to give the child a firmer belief in his uniqueness and goodness and his value to us.

The fifth goal is to build up between us and our child an atmosphere of equality of persons. To sense the equality of persons is a terribly important goal. All of us realize how difficult it is to treat the child as an equal no matter how honestly and sincerely we may attempt to do so. However, if we face into the child as an expression of our relationship with one another and as the gift of our husband or wife to us, then there's no teacher-pupil, no superior-inferior attitude in our minds. The child assumes the dignity and the worth of the husband or the wife.

The sixth goal, also of tremendous importance, is for children themselves to know their value. Constantly our young people are asking themselves, "What's my worth, what's the reason for my existence?" The simplest answer and yet the deepest and only believable answer that can give them any true sense of value is simply and solely, "You are what we mean to one another. The whole reason for your existence is to express the magnificence of our love. There can be no greater calling in life. It's not just anybody's love. It's not love in general. It's the specific love we—your mother and father —have for one another. We are unique, our love is totally special and irreplaceable, and so are you—the child of our love who speaks it."

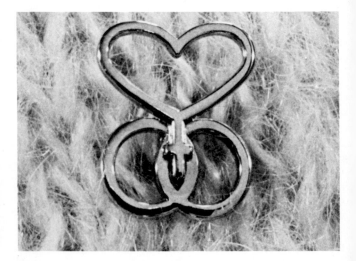